THE
HENDERSON'S
RELISH
COOKBOOK

HENDERSON'S
RELISH COOKBOOK

©2015 Meze Publishing & Henderson's Relish.
All rights reserved.
Second edition printed in 2015 in the UK.

ISBN: 978-0-9928981-3-7

Written: Pamela Freeman, Joe Food

Edited: Joe Food, Phil Turner

Proofed: James Highmore, Rachel Heward

Cover: Pete McKee

Photography: Marc Barker

Additional Photography: Timm Cleasby, Tim Green,
Matt Brewin, Paul Cocker

Design: Paul Cocker

Contributors: Simon Freeman, Julia Waxman,
Patrick Byrne, Liz Castleton, Nick Hallam,
Carl Reid, Sarah Koriba, Faye Bailey

Published by Meze Publishing Limited
Unit 1 Beehive Works
Milton Street
Sheffield S3 7WL
www.mezepublishing.co.uk
Tel: 0114 275 7709

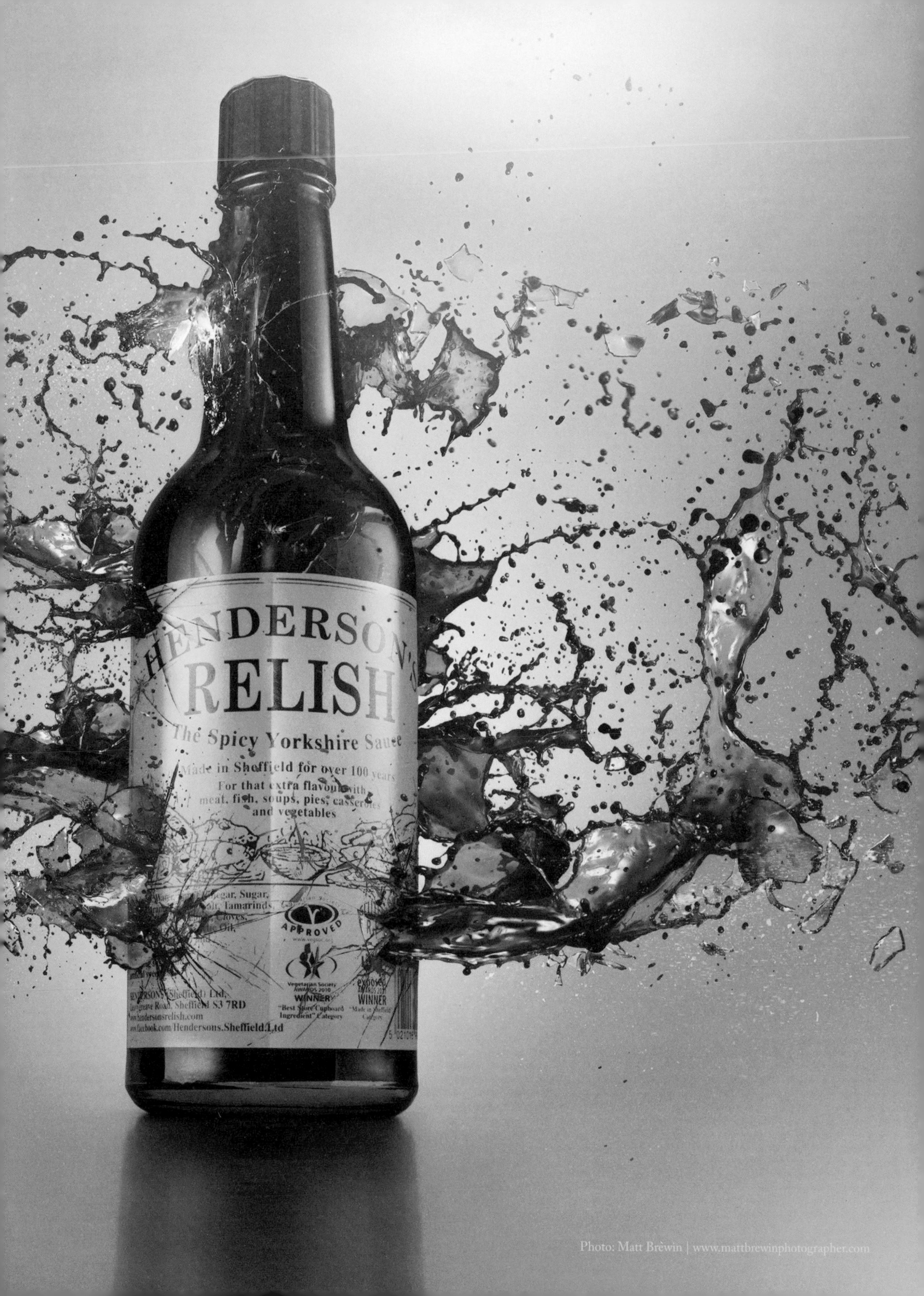

Photo: Matt Brewin | www.mattbrewinphotographer.com

The FOREWORD

WE'RE VERY PROUD OF OUR RELISH AND THE WAY PEOPLE HAVE
TAKEN IT TO THEIR HEARTS. WE HOPE YOU ENJOY THIS BOOK.

This company has been part of the Freeman family for roughly 75 years, having been passed down from husbands to wives, sisters to brothers and aunties to nephews. We are immensely proud to call it a family business and it gives me great pleasure to know that it will continue to remain within our care when the company is passed down to my children, Simon and Julia.

We remain forever dedicated to preserving the integrity of the brand and the secret mix will continue to be carefully guarded, retaining the sense of mystery which makes our product so unique.

First of all, I would like to dedicate this book to my late husband, Dr Kenneth Freeman. The company was still very small when it came under our care in 1991, but he had enough belief in both the product and himself to take the business to where it is at the present time. There is no doubt in my mind that we would not be where we are today without the hard work and devotion he gave to the company and the brand. Since my husband's family were all born and bred Sheffield folk, I daresay he understood better than anyone the importance of the product to the local people.

With that in mind, we would also like to send our deepest gratitude to the people of Sheffield for their continuing loyalty to Henderson's Relish. We are overawed and honoured at the level of pride the city takes in the brand and hope that this book goes some way to repaying their dedication by providing them with new means to continue spicing up their food.

Finally, I would like to say that we are both humbled and delighted to be considered a piece of Sheffield's culture and history for over 125 years and remain committed to providing culinary delight to its wonderful supporters, now, and for future generations.

Pamela Freeman

Managing Director of Henderson's (Sheffield) Ltd.

The CONTENTS

THE HISTORY OF HENDERSON'S RELISH

The Foreword   4

The History of
Henderson's Relish   10

Henry Henderson   14

Charles Hinksman   18

Dr Kenneth Freeman   22

The Hawley Years   24

Hendogate   28

Henderson's Relish on Tour   30

The New Factory   34

CULTURAL ICONS

Pete McKee   50

Kid Acne   58

Shaun Doane   66

Lisa Maltby   76

Matt Brewin   84

Sam Bajdala-Cressey   92

Katey Felton   100

Matt Cockayne   108

Jim Connolly   118

Mark Musgrave   126

Luke Prest   138

Richard Hawley   144

James Coates   154

RECIPES

Henderson's Relish family pie   40

Henderson's marinated beef
with Asian spring roll   42

David Blunkett's shepherd's pie   44

Vanilla cheesecake
with black cherry ripple   46

Beefburger with tomato ketchup   60

Triple-decker fried egg sandwich   62

Swede & celeriac pakoras   64

Steak & Henderson's pasty   68

Ashoka house puri   70

Cheese & bacon muffins   72

Chocolate & Hendo's mousse   74

Tomato chilli pickle   78

Braised beef cheeks
with crispy fried oyster   80

Walnut & seed salad toppers   82

Chocolate pave
with pink peppercorn strawberries   86

Black bean & soya burger   88

Vegetarian shepherd's pie   90

The Laundrette bloody Marys   94

Henderson's & black treacle
cured salmon   96

Blue cheese mousse
with Lord Marples bread   98

Ox tail cottage pie   102

Corned beef hash potato cake
with soft poached egg   104

Henderson's chocolate truffles   106

Trojan Boss beef stew   110

Nick Clegg's pasta bake   112

Cheese on toast, toast on cheese   114

Bloody Mary & crab cannelloni   120

Smoked bacon hashcake
with fried duck egg   122

Cherries four-ways
with Henderson's ice cream   124

Jon McClure's Chilli Con Carne   128

Yorkshire brisket
with Henderson's gravy   130

Mushroom meringue
with summer fruits   132

Chocolate courgette cake   134

Sausage casserole   140

Steak burger   142

Sheffield secret mixed grill   150

Slow cooked ox cheek   152

Cliff House mushroom stack   156

Marinated stawberries
with pistachio cake   158

EST^D 1885

"The Yorkshire Original"

HENDERSON'S RELISH

'Hendo's', 'the Black Stuff', 'Relish' is today a Sheffield institution, adding spice and savour to any dish. Splash it on Rarebit, stir it in Shepherd's Pie, teem it into your Bloody Mary, tip it over Fish and Chips for a fuller, richer flavour.

Henry Henderson

Made in Sheffield, to a secret recipe

ERSON'S

LISH

Soups, Fish & Game

per, Tamarinds, Saccharin,
d Cayenne Pepper, Cloves,
ment and Malt Vinegar.

HE BOTTLE

(Sheffield) LTD.
Road, Sheffield

Maximum
Retail Price **9p**

DERS

ELISH

2D. BOT

THE BOT

Gravies, Soups,

MANUFACTURE

ENDER

VE ROAD, S

ERSON'S

LISH

Soups, Fish & G

BOTT

(Sheffield) LTD

7

The History of HENDERSON'S RELISH

MADE IN SHEFFIELD FOR OVER 100 YEARS

First of all, on behalf of the team behind the Henderson's Cookbook, we would like to congratulate you on purchasing a valuable piece of Sheffield history. In a city which has given the world so much in the form of manufacturing, music, film, art and sport – Henderson's Relish remains a main source (or should that be 'sauce'?) of admiration for Sheffielders. It embodies the very essence of what makes the city great. It is the cultural lifeblood behind its character.

Yet, the city's most famous culinary export has always been shrouded in a sense of mystery. What actually went on behind those old factory doors? What dishes would the sauce supplement over 100 years ago? How does one set about unravelling the complex family lineage – from Henry Henderson's late 19th century breakthrough, to the company entering the care of Dr Freeman in 1991?

Unfortunately, we can't promise that we'll be able to answer all of your questions (the secret recipe remains off limits!) But we can take a comprehensive look into the past, present and potential future adventures of Yorkshire's best kept secret.

Feeling comfortable? Let's roll back the years. All the way back to 1885…

Queen Victoria was on the throne; whilst professional football had only recently been legalised (if only they knew of the suffering which Sheffield football supporters would endure over the following 130 years!) The large borough of Sheffield (not yet granted city status) was frequently blanketed by industrial smog, as the old town moved to the beating sounds of grinding mills, steelwork factories and cutlery workshops. Yet, inside a small general merchant store situated on Broad Lane, Henry Henderson had just perfected a spicy formula which would grow to become a staple part of everyday life for generations of Sheffield families.

Henry
HENDERSON

IN THE BEGINNING GOD CREATED THE HEAVEN AND THE EARTH AND
HENRY HENDERSON CREATED OUR RELISH.

Nobody quite knows the precise moment or date when Henry Henderson discovered the recipe for a product which would go on to gain cult-like success in his city. In his occupation as a dry salter and wholesale chemist, he would blend ingredients to create various mixtures which he would then sell from his General Merchant Store, situated at 35 Broad Lane (roughly where The University of Sheffield accommodation stands today.) Initially, the sauce was kept inside a large barrel within the store and this is how Henderson's Relish was born. As word of a new spicy sauce spread throughout the city, local shoppers began to visit the store with small glass bottles at hand, seeking their fill.

The product was a success from the beginning; Henderson's continued to sell barrel after barrel of their condiment until 1910, the year in which a pickle manufacturing company called Shaws of Huddersfield saw enough potential to make Henderson an offer to purchase the business. The bid was accepted, and the company moved less than half a mile up the street to their second address at 66 Leavygreave Road.

Back in the early 1900s, people were much more economical when it came to waste; small Henderson's bottles would be saved after use then taken to the factory for refills by prudent Sheffielders – bearing in mind that, due to its one penny (1d) price tag, the condiment would almost have been classed as a delicacy back then. Even in recent times, Henderson's staff claim to have received visits to the factory from older members of the Sheffield community asking whether they could bring their old bottle in for a refill.

Some of the bottles from the early 20th century would have had the words 'suitable for soups, fish and game' written across the front. 'Game', of course, referring to animals which had been hunted for food; back in those days, popular game meat in Sheffield would have included rabbit, grouse or pheasant. Once again, for the sake of frugality, the original bottles were made much smaller in those days – some only holding an estimated 100ml of relish, which isn't much when compared to the 284ml capacity of modern bottles.

Charles
HINKSMAN

WE OWE OUR THANKS TO CHARLES HINKSMAN FOR OUR ICONIC OLD FACTORY

George Shaw's daughter Miriam was married to a gentleman called Charles William Hinksman, who also hailed from Huddersfield but moved to Sheffield around the year 1911. In 1940, the company became limited in its own right as Hinksman bought the company from Shaws. Charles Hinksman became Managing Director of the company around that time. In 1959, the company was incorporated as Henderson's (Sheffield) Limited – which still exists in the same form today.

It was during Mr Hinksman's tenure that the decision was made to move premises to the now iconic Sheffield address of number 41 Leavygreave Road – instantly recognisable by thousands as the "old Henderson's factory." Its modest, traditional appearance saw the building find its way into the hearts of many. Over the years, it grew to become a symbolic city landmark – even today it still manages to turn the heads of local residents driving past, or those wandering into the city centre for a weekly shop or a pint.

One of the main charms with the old factory was the mystery which surrounded what went on behind those closed doors. Local legend dictates that not a single person could be seen entering or leaving the premises during working hours. The size of the building didn't make much sense, either; just how could they fit all of those bottles and a factory inside such a small space? Fables of a northern Oompa-Loompa workforce and a building with Tardis-like capabilities were passed down through generations of curious families from the city.

Miriam Hinksman (nee Shaw) passed away in 1939, and Charles Hinksman later remarried Gladys Freeman – the aunt of the late Dr Kenneth Freeman. After Charles Hinksman's death, the company was given to Gladys, and has remained in the hands of the Freeman family ever since. Gladys Freeman passed the reins over to her more business-savvy brother, Harvey Freeman, who ran the company until his passing in 1984, which saw tenure pass over to his wife Connie Freeman – previously a headmistress from Dore – who continued to run the business for seven years.

Dr Kenneth
FREEMAN

DR FREEMAN ELEVATED HENDERSON'S RELISH FROM A FAMILIAR LOCAL
CONDIMENT – TO LEGENDARY STATUS IN ITS HOME CITY.

In 1991, ownership of the company was passed from Connie Freeman to her nephew, Dr Kenneth Freeman. Along with his wife Pamela, Dr Freeman would oversee ground-breaking developments in the company's profile.

In those days, Henderson's Relish only distributed to one supermarket – the Co-op.

A Land Rover would pull up outside the factory twice a week and ten or twenty cases would be stacked into the boot before the delivery person would go off on their rounds – mostly delivering to various corner shops around the city. Dr Freeman, accompanied by his wife, would visit various supermarket chains carrying a bottle of Henderson's to pitch to potential buyers. At first, it made for quite a contrasting experience for Kenneth Freeman who had spent the last 45 years as a doctor in general practice. However, the hard work eventually paid off and Sainsbury's became the company's largest supermarket partner in 1996. From that point on, the product started to sell itself as more local supermarkets came on board; Henderson's Relish became much more accessible for its adoring Sheffield audience and word began to spread a bit further afield, adding to its already substantial fan base.

The success of Henderson's in its hometown had previously been a rather modest, understated affair; by their very nature, Sheffield people are not the type to openly blow their own trumpet. Yet, over the last decade, the current owners of the company will tell you that they have seen a huge growth in the 'cult status' of the product.

There are a number of theories to what may have contributed to the phenomenal rise in displays of Henderson's fandom. Some put it down to a mixture of local pride and nostalgia, or the lack of original locally produced products in today's marketplace. However, one thing is for certain: a company which seldom spends on advertising has benefited with a helping hand from a selection of famous fans singing its praises over the years.

The HAWLEY YEARS

Out of a long list of celebrities to fly the flag for the Henderson's brand, Richard Hawley was the first to openly profess his admiration for the sauce to a wider audience. Born in the Sheffield suburb of Pitsmoor, Richard found widescale recognition in the 1990's as a member of The Longpigs, later joining up with fellow Sheffield compatriot Jarvis Cocker for a short time in Pulp. After Pulp split up in 2000, Richard embarked on a successful solo career – going on to release seven studio albums as of 2014.

Richard has spoken fondly of his relationship with the brand in various interviews – recounting how a sprinkle of Henderson's can remind him of home, or provide comfort after a long time on the road. In 2001, he held a party in the factory yard to celebrate the launch of his self-titled first album, Richard Hawley. He was also the first to kick off something of a trend after commissioning his own limited edition bottle – promoting his 2005 Mercury Prize nominated album, Coles Corner. In 2007, another label was produced to celebrate his album, Lady's Bridge – using the album cover itself to decorate the bottle. Such bottles would be sold after live performances up and down the country.

But it was a certain young band from High Green, Sheffield, who managed to nab Richard Hawley's 2005 Mercury Prize nomination. The Arctic Monkeys won the award and famously declared, "Somebody call 999 - Richard Hawley has been robbed." Since the release of their first album in 2006, the band has gone on to become one of the biggest UK indie-rock acts since the heyday of Oasis. Despite their meteoric rise, the band have remained faithful to their Henderson's roots, with drummer Matt Helders once saying during an interview in The Guardian "Do you know what Henderson's Relish is? ... It's like Worcester Sauce but a million times better," and later adding that he packs four bottles in his suitcase before leaving on a tour. Lead singer Alex Turner has also been known to bemoan the lack of Henderson's Relish whilst touring abroad during interviews.

In 2013, the band cemented their affection for the sauce by bringing out their own commissioned label to celebrate the release of their fifth studio album, AM. The band's manager, Geoff Barradale, personally visited the factory to work on the label and collect the finished product.

Other notable celebrities to commission their own labels include DJ Toddla T, who produced his 'Dubplate' Henderson's bottle – the 'Steel City Soundboy Edition.' Meanwhile, local artist and Henderson's enthusiast, Pete Mckee has had two separate labels printed, which celebrate his Month of Sundays gallery and the Tour de Yorkshire-inspired King of The Hills series.

Even Sheffield's largest musical festival got in on the action when they produced their own labels to celebrate the 2014 headliners; Katy Bean, Pub Lunch Enemy and Annie Mac 'n' Cheese were designed by Peter & Paul, and the bottles went down a treat amongst festival goers who purchased from various outlets around the city over Tramlines weekend.

RSON'S
LISH

NIE
CHEE

P

TRAMLINES MUS

HENDERSON'S RELISH

THE SPICY YORKSHIRE SAUCE

UB LUNC
ENEMY

ESTIVAL

HENDOGATE

WHEN SHEFFIELD ROSE TO THE DEFENCE OF ITS FAVOURITE SAUCE.

In January 2014, Labour MP Jim Dowd whipped up quite a storm amongst Henderson's lovers after making some misjudged (to say the least) comments about the brand during a House of Commons speech. Unsurprisingly, the uproar from Sheffielders was a sight to behold. The MP for Lewisham West and Penge was left dumbstruck as he received a huge backlash of angry emails and letters demanding an apology. Even Deputy Prime Minister Nick Clegg got involved with the scandal through sending an open letter to his fellow MP, asking him to reconsider his comments on a 'much loved local institution.'

As ever, the Henderson's team remained humble throughout the affair. Director, Simon Freeman attempted to quell the furore in an amicable manner by inviting Mr Dowd up to Sheffield for a visit to the factory and, of course, a meat pie covered in Henderson's Relish. Thankfully, he accepted the offer and spent a day in Sheffield learning about the history of Henderson's, the deep association the product has with local people and (perhaps most importantly) its superior taste. After being treated to the full Henderson's experience, Mr Dowd admitted that he had made something of a gaffe and retracted his original comments. The company itself gained a new supporter and the Henderson's faithful could sleep easier knowing that its good name had been protected.

Henderson's Relish
ON TOUR

FROM SHEFFIELD TO SINGAPORE ... AUSTRALIA ... CANADA ... DUBAI,
HENDERSON'S RELISH IS CERTAINLY WELL-TRAVELLED

In fact, it's a bit of a myth that you can only purchase Henderson's Relish within South Yorkshire these days. Shops stocking Henderson's can be found as far away as Whitby, Filey, Scotland and, yes, even "that-there London!"

Bottles of Henderson's Relish are distributed around the world on a regular basis. Whilst filming Sharpe in 2008, Sean Bean once ordered a batch of Henderson's to his film set in India. Dubai DJ, Catboy, orders a bottle or two on a regular basis – once inviting celebrity chef Marco Pierre White to try some Henderson's live on air. Of course, Marco loved it and has remarked since that he'd certainly consider adding the relish to one of his future dishes.

In 2009, Dr Freeman decided to send out a few one litre sized bottles of Henderson's to troops in Afganistan. And, in 2014, more giant bottles were sent out to a Sheffield soldier at the request of his wife – inadvertently managing to convert an entire platoon into Henderson's addicts by doing so!

Customers in Singapore, Australia, the Falkland Islands and even Hong Kong have all been in touch with the Henderson's Relish sales department. Families have been known to send bottles over to their fellow kin living in countries such as the US, New Zealand, Spain and Canada. It's fair to say that despite its local connotations, Hendo's certainly gets around!

The new FACTORY

November 2013 marked the end of an era for Henderson's Relish as the company moved from the humble yet iconic Leavygreave Road building to new premises at Sheffield Parkway Business Park. Even though it was a difficult choice to make, the move was necessary if the company was to continue satisfying consumer demand for the sauce. Also vital to the move was the desire to achieve the SALSA accreditation (Safe and Local Supplier Approval) which will allow the company to sell the product to new supermarkets around the UK – slowly spreading the word of the relish. Unfortunately, spatial and architectural issues at the old building would have made it very challenging to achieve the aforementioned accreditation.

Owner, Pamela Freeman believes that the move to the new factory was the right thing to do for the brand.

"We had a review done at the old factory building; it soon became clear that we had to start looking at replacing the walls, ceilings and floors before looking at anything else. Unfortunately, it would have required a large amount of money to be able to carry on with the old building. The new unit was built to the correct standards with greater storage. Overall, we now have more room, more glass and bigger vats – which means more Henderson's!"

More Henderson's indeed; the move to the new factory has allowed the company to significantly increase production.

Pat Byrne, General Manager of Henderson's joined in March 2014. He is confident about the bright future which lies in store for the brand but also recognises the importance of continuing to celebrate its Sheffield roots:

"We now have the opportunity to grow as a business; but we also need to focus on the brand's fine heritage and continue to pay back the warmth and support shown to us by local people."

A product which began life in such humble fashion over a century ago has since endured two world wars, a large scale Blitz, numerous periods of economic depression and even had its own MP scandal to contend with. Throughout it all, Henderson's Relish remains an honest family run business with deep roots and pride in the Sheffield community which has served it so well for over a century. From the days of Henry Henderson to the late Dr Freeman, the brand has always been handled properly with utmost care and genuine affection for the product. Its success has seen it established as nothing short of an institution in Sheffield – adorning the kitchen tables and cupboard shelves of families from South Yorkshire for generations.

Exciting times are ahead for Henderson's Relish. With its new premises and increased manufacturing power, the company today has more potential than ever before to spread culinary delight and perhaps begin to convert even more people to the Henderson's way of life. It's only fair that we Sheffielders live up to our name as friendly folk and help to share Yorkshire's best kept secret far and wide. Because it would be selfish to keep it all to ourselves now, wouldn't it?

DERSON'S
ELISH

y Yorkshire Sauce

effield for over 100 years

ur with meat, fish, soups
les and vegetables

ugar,
rinds,

Vegetarian Society
APPROVED
www.vegsoc.org

GLUTEN FREE

ENDERSON'S
RELISH

he Spicy Yorkshire Sauce

Made in Sheffield for over 100 years

tra flavour with meat, fish, soups
casseroles and vegetables

Vinegar, Sugar,
Salt, Tamarinds,
Pepper, Cloves,
Garlic Oil,
and

SHAKE TH
28
10
Best Be

APPROVED
www.vegsoc.org

GLUTEN FREE

field) Ltd,
field S9 4WQ

dersons.Sheffield.Ltd

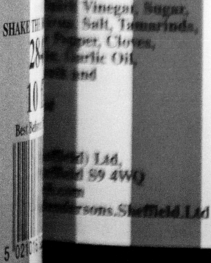
5 021018

field.Ltd

HENDERSON'S RELISH
FAMILY PIE

THIS IS THE PIE THAT OUR FRIENDS AT THE RUTLAND HOTEL SERVED TO JIM DOWD MP
ON HIS VISIT TO THE HENDERSON'S FACTORY. SERVES 4

INGREDIENTS

For the rough puff pastry

225g plain flour

½ tsp fine salt

250g unsalted butter, cold but not rock hard (or you can use half butter & lard)

150ml ice-cold water

1 free-range egg, beaten, to glaze

For the filling

1kg braising steak, cut into matchbox-sized pieces

3 tbsp plain flour

Salt and freshly ground black pepper

3 tbsp olive oil

300ml Kelham Island beer

2 garlic cloves

2 onions

Handful fresh thyme sprigs

300ml good quality beef stock

1 tbsp tomato purée

6 tbsp Henderson's Relish

50g butter

METHOD

To make the pastry, sift the flour and salt into a large mixing bowl. Place in the fridge for a few minutes to chill.

Cube the butter and stir into a bowl until each piece is well-coated with flour. Add the water, then, working quickly; use a knife to bring everything together to a rough dough.

Gather the dough and then turn it onto a work surface. Squash the dough into a fat, flat sausage, without kneading. Wrap in cling film then chill in the fridge for 15 minutes.

Lightly flour the work surface and pastry. Roll out the pastry in one direction until it is around 1cm thick and three times as long as it is wide. Straighten up the sides keeping the top & bottom edges as square as possible.

Fold the bottom third of the pastry up, then the top third down, to make a block – the important thing is that the corners are nice and square.

Roll out and fold again, repeating this four times in all.

Chill the finished pastry for an hour, or ideally overnight before using.

For the filling, mix the beef with the flour, salt and pepper.

Heat the oil in a large casserole dish to a medium heat, shake off the excess flour from the beef and fry for 10 minutes, until golden brown all over.

Transfer the meat to a bowl and add the beer, Henderson's Relish and stock.

Chop the garlic and onion into chunky pieces. Add the meat and herbs to the pan and fry to soften for a few minutes.

Add the tomato purée, cover and simmer the stew for 1-1½ hours until the beef is almost tender and the sauce has thickened. Cool overnight if possible.

Melt the butter in a large frying pan then add to the cooled pie filling and add to the pie dish.

To make the pie, preheat the oven to 200°C. Roll out the pastry to the thickness of two £1 coins and wide enough for the pie dish with some excess.

Use a sharp knife to cut the pastry – if it's too big it doesn't matter. Lay the pastry over a rolling pin to lift it on to the pie. Press down gently to seal.

Holding the knife blade horizontally, make a patterned edge by pressing down gently all around the edge of the pastry (this will help the layers in the pastry to puff up).

Cut a couple of slits in the top of the pie to release the steam while cooking.

Bake for 30 minutes, or until the filling is bubbling and the pastry is golden-brown and puffed all over.

JASON HORTON - THE RUTLAND HOTEL

Situated just over a mile away from the city centre in the leafy suburb of Broomhall, The Rutland Hotel has blended traditional Victorian character with contemporary design to create the perfect place for special occasions in Sheffield. Their steak and Henderson's pie has grown to become a firm favourite amongst restaurant visitors – including one MP who ate a rather large slice of humble pie at the venue.

HENDERSON'S MARINATED BEEF WITH ASIAN SPRING ROLL

THE SPICY TAMARIND IN HENDERSON'S RELISH WORKS WELL WITH ASIAN FLAVOURS.
SERVES 2

INGREDIENTS

2 x 125g beef medallions
For the marinade
1 lime leaf, shredded
1 lemongrass stalk, outer skin removed &
finely chopped
1 clove garlic, finely chopped
Small piece ginger, finely chopped
100ml Henderson's Relish
For the spring rolls
50g black pudding, finely chopped
1 tsp Henderson's Relish
1 egg, for the eggwash
2 spring roll wrappers
For the Asian pesto
50g cashew nuts
50g coriander
25g mint & chervil
40g Parmesan cheese, finely grated
1 piece fresh ginger, chopped
1 clove garlic
1 red chilli, de-seeded, chopped
1 tbsp lime juice
4 tbsp olive oil
For the salad
Bean sprouts
Mooli, finely sliced
Red pepper, finely sliced
Spring onion, finely sliced
Micro-coriander
Squeeze lime juice
Salt

METHOD

Combine all the ingredients and marinate the beef in the marinade for at least 1 hour.

For the pesto

Whiz the cashew nuts, garlic and ginger in a blender for 1 minute, add the herbs and chilli then whiz again until smooth.

Add olive oil and lime juice, fold in Parmesan cheese and season.

For the spring rolls

Mix the black pudding and Henderson's Relish together to form a paste.

Place equal amounts of the mixture in the middle of each spring roll wrapper, brush the edges with eggwash and seal the spring rolls.

To serve

Pat the fillets dry, then fry in a hot pan until cooked to your preference.

Deep-fry the spring rolls until golden brown and drain on kitchen paper.

Place the beef medallions in the centre of a plate.

Place on a spring roll and a spoon of Asian pesto over the beef.

Combine all the salad items together and arrange on the plate.

ANDY GABBITAS - THE WORTLEY ARMS

Sheffield-born Andy Gabbitas is a classically-trained chef who has been cooking for nearly 40 years and has been a Master Chef of Great Britain for over 10 of them.

Bringing a wealth of international experience to the table, having served in the Army Catering Corps and as a private chef on yachts, his career has taken him as far afield as Hong Kong, Belize, New Zealand and Canada.

Andy is an avid Sheffield Wednesday fan, with a huge collection of memorabilia on display in his pub.

DAVID BLUNKETT'S
SHEPHERD'S PIE

DAVID MADE THIS RECIPE WHEN HE APPEARED AS A CELEBRITY CHEF ON THE TV
SHOW 'THE F WORD' – COOKING AGAINST THE MAN HIMSELF, GORDON RAMSAY.

INGREDIENTS

450g minced lamb

4 large potatoes

2 carrots, finely diced

2 onions, sliced

225g mushrooms

½ tin peeled tomatoes

1 garlic clove, chopped

1 pint lamb stock

Salt and black pepper

1 tsp sugar

A generous slug of Henderson's Relish

1 tbsp oil

1 knob butter

Grated cheese for topping

METHOD

Peel and dice the potatoes. To a saucepan of boiling water, add a little salt, and gently boil the potatoes until cooked but still firm. Leave to stand with the lid on.

Slice the onions, crush the garlic then fry gently in tablespoon of oil in a large deep frying pan. When they start to soften and become transparent, add one teaspoon of sugar and a tablespoon of water and stir well. The onions will then soon become soft and caramelised.

While this is cooking, peel and chop the carrots into small pieces and add to the frying pan.

Add the minced lamb to the pan and gently fry for 2 minutes, then add a generous slug of Henderson's Relish.

Add the lamb stock and begin to simmer on a very low heat.

Add the peeled tomatoes to the pan and continue to simmer.

Slice the mushrooms and cook separately in a little butter in a small frying pan, adding black pepper.

When the meat and carrots are cooked, after about 25 minutes, add the mushrooms and remove from heat.

Put the mixture into a casserole dish. Try the taste test at this point and add more seasoning if necessary. Don't add all the liquid as this will soak into the potatoes and make them too mushy.

Mash the cooked potatoes with some butter but keeping the mash quite firm, and spread over the mixture.

Cook for a further 20 minutes in a hot oven at 190°C.

Finish with some grated cheese on top, or for an interesting variation, why not mash some cooked swede or celeriac into the potato top.

Serve with a dash of Henderson's Relish.

THE RT. HON. DAVID BLUNKETT MP

Born at Jessop Hospital – a short stroll away from the old Henderson's factory – David Blunkett grew up in Sheffield. After graduating from Sheffield University with a degree in Political Theory and Institutions, he entered local politics, and at the age of 22, became the youngest ever councillor in Britain. Elected as Labour MP for Sheffield Brightside during the 1987 general election, he has held the seat since. In 1992 he joined the shadow cabinet as Shadow Health Secretary, later going on to hold the positions of Secretary of State for Education and Home Secretary.

Vanilla Cheesecake with
Black Cherry Ripple

THE SOUR CHEESE AND SWEET HENDERSON'S RELISH
REDUCTION GIVES THIS CHEESECAKE A LOVELY DECADENT TASTE

Ingredients

For the cheesecake filling

250g cream cheese, full fat

30g icing sugar

2 large vanilla pods, seeds scraped out

200ml double cream, semi-whipped

4 egg yolks

30g caster sugar

2 gelatine leaves

For the ripple

140g fresh black cherries

100ml Henderson's Relish

25ml balsamic vinegar

125g Muscovado sugar

50ml black cherry juice

For the cheesecake base

200g Amaretti biscuits

50g melted unsalted butter

Method

To start place the Henderson's relish, balsamic vinegar, black cherries and juice and Muscovado sugar in a saucepan and put on a low heat. Leave to simmer until reduced to a syrup.

While the Henderson's is reducing, put the egg yolks and caster sugar in a bowl and whisk until pale in colour and it has become light and fluffy.

Put the cream cheese in a bowl with the icing sugar and stir until soft.

Soak the gelatine leaves in cold water.

Soft whip the double cream with the vanilla seeds (it should be smooth and glossy not firm and grainy.)

Melt the gelatine in a small saucepan with a couple of tablespoons of water. Once melted, whisk the gelatine into the sabayon very quickly until it is all mixed in. Fold in the cream cheese. Fold in the whipped cream.

Strain the reduction and keep the cherries for finishing. Using a pastry brush, line a piping bag with the syrup and then fill with the cheesecake mixture ready for use.

Making the base

Place the biscuits in a clean tea towel and softly tap them with the rolling pin until crumbled. Then place into a bowl with the melted butter. Mix together well and spoon into four ring moulds and press down with a spoon. Refrigerate the bases for 10 minutes before piping in the cheesecake mixture.

To finish

Pipe your cheesecake mixture into the ring moulds right to the top and refrigerate until set, for approximately 2-3 hours. Once set, remove the cheesecakes from the refrigerator and warm the ring with a blow torch, or warm with a hot cloth, for 2-3 seconds, then lift off the ring with a towel. Garnish with your black cherries and dust with icing. Serve with fresh cream if desired.

SIMON AYRES

Dubbed by Gordon Ramsay as "the cage fighter in the kitchen", Simon previously worked at the acclaimed Milestone restaurant which reached the semi-final stage of Ramsay's Best Restaurant in 2010. Now head chef at the Showroom Workstation on Paternoster Row, Simon has overseen a revamp of the menu that places a renewed focus on fresh, local food of the highest quality.

Cultural
ICONS

NOT MANY FOODS BECOME CULTURAL ICONS, LET ALONE INSPIRE SONGS AND
WORKS OF ART. 'HENDERSON'S RELISH' – YORKSHIRE'S BEST KEPT SECRET.

Over the years, Henderson's Relish has provided the key ingredient for various food dishes, but it has also inspired incredible works of art, music and literature. In this section we show how the product went from condiment to cultural icon.

WHAT'S FOR TEA?

MONDAY HASH

TUESDAY TOAD INT HOLE

WEDNESDAY SAUS MASH

THURSDAY PIE

FRIDAY CHIPPIE

SATURDAY COTTAGE PIE

SUNDAY BEEF

SUMMAT WI.... RELISH

Art: Matt Cockayne | goo-design.myshopify.com

Art: Luke Prest | www.lukeprest.com

Pete MCKEE

SHEFFIELD-LAD PETE HAS HAD A RELATIONSHIP WITH HENDERSON'S RELISH
SINCE CHILDHOOD, LEADING HIM TO PRODUCE SEVERAL KEY PIECES OF
HENDO'S ART OVER THE YEARS

"I first developed my style of painting in 2005; I began by painting my personal recollections and experiences of Sheffield. If I was painting a kitchen scene, I would always ensure that there was a Henderson's Relish bottle in there somewhere. The Hendo's would serve as the visual cue that the painting featured a Sheffield household; the bottle wouldn't always be at the centre of attention, but as a quiet constant in the background."

If you were to visit Pete McKee's Month of Sundays gallery on Sharrow Vale Road, you would find yourself stood amongst something of a homage to Sheffield history, lifestyle and culture. Notable footballers from both sides of the city, past and present musical icons, and city landmarks hang on the walls while various examples of local memorabilia such as an old Stones Bitter pump and, of course, limited edition Henderson's Relish bottles are also on show. Over time, his artwork and various projects have helped him to become a Sheffield icon in his own right; examples of his work hang proudly in the homes of many Sheffielders and collaborations with the likes of Noel Gallagher, Arctic Monkeys, Disney and Paul Smith have helped him establish a growing international fanbase.

As a devout Sheffielder his childhood memories play a key role in some of his work and what collection of childhood remembrances is complete for any Sheffielder without early memories of the Henderson's Relish experience?

"I'll always remember the original metal top which came with the bottles. Back then, you'd have to pierce the top with a sharp knife and shake out the relish like vinegar. You'd have a bottle of Henderson's kicking around the kitchen with a bit of crusty, dried up Henderson's on top. I also remember being a kid and getting a meat and potato pie put in front of you with the thickest crust on earth. The only way we could moisten the huge crust would be to soak it in relish."

It's clear that McKee is immensely proud of his Sheffield roots. He describes Sheffield as a city of "Little Mesters" – a local term for highly skilled craftspeople who were either self-employed or working as part of a small team. During the late 1800's, such workers were instrumental in establishing Sheffield's reputation in cutlery and tool-making. Pete believes that the city's proud history in local production and creativity goes some way to explaining the affection that Sheffielders hold for home-grown brands such as Henderson's.

Pete McKee
canvas prints

Small prints £60

Large prints £120

"We're still very proud of the things we self-produce. It's instilled in the psyche of the city's people. Henderson's Relish has become a real cultural icon over the last five or six years; I recall Kid Acne as being the first person to celebrate it in an artistic sense and that side has certainly taken off."

The artist has featured Henderson's Relish in his work on a number of occasions, previously decorating a bottle with Swarovski jewels to create "The World's Most Expensive Henderson's Bottle" and once suspending a bottle in formaldehyde as a tongue-in-cheek reference to Damien Hirst. But it's the "Holy Watter" piece – the first painting to feature a bottle of Henderson's on its own – which has become a particular favourite with fans of the sauce. To give the piece a bit of character, Pete created his own bit of Henderson's mythology – claiming that the painting was inspired by a lost tattoo design found on a scrap of paper in an old Sheffield outhouse. However, the story later came to life as he was informed that an admirer of the painting used the design for a real tattoo!

The mystery behind the Henderson's brand has made it all the more endearing to him; he fondly recalls visiting the old factory on Leavygreave Road and meeting the late Dr Freeman:

"There was always a bit of a Willy Wonka aspect with the old factory; there would be stories that you could sit outside of the gates all day and never see anybody go in or out – and, to be fair, you never did! But I think that intrigue is part of what makes it so popular. I recollect that Dr Freeman was very protective and careful with the brand – a huge level of concern went into it."

Pete has acknowledged the close ties between Henderson's Relish and Sheffield in his art by choosing the distinctive shade of orange used on the labels as the colour of Sheffield – using it to highlight specific references to the city. Much of his Sheffield related artwork deals with nostalgia and a sense of civic identity – something he believes the city has always held in abundance but hasn't necessarily promoted until recently.

"You see, creating Sheffield as a brand is a fairly recent development. We've always been proud of our city, but it's not until recent times that we've become very vocal about that pride. I think once you started to get people such as Jarvis Cocker and Richard Hawley openly mentioning Sheffield in their songs and interviews, we all realised that we could start to shout about the place a bit more. As a family run business, Henderson's Relish has that strong sense of uniqueness which people from the city love."

That sense of uniqueness is key to what he calls the "cultural importance" of Henderson's to its home city. He concedes that he can get slightly evangelical when it comes to introducing people to the product for the first time; then again, from somebody who shares his experiences and passion for Sheffield through his art, that is surely to be expected. However, somewhat surprisingly, McKee also admits to being quite sparing in his personal use of the condiment, describing himself as a "Hendo's traditionalist" – he saves the relish for use on one fundamental dish: meat and tatty pie.

Kid ACNE

KNOWN FOR HIS INNOVATION, KID ACNE IS WIDELY ACKNOWLEDGED AS THE
FIRST ARTIST TO PRESENT A PIECE FEATURING HENDERSON'S RELISH

Kid Acne is an artist, illustrator and occasionally an MC based in Sheffield. He is perhaps best known locally for his many street art installations located around the city centre, one example being the "You'll Thank Me One Day" slogan featured on the side of the former Sheffield Independent Film building near Brown Street. Today his work can be seen both inside and outside galleries across the world, while some of his illustrations have been used by famous brands such as Prada, Kenzo, and Elle.

He has also released a variety of music records, most notably his critically acclaimed 2007 album Romance Ain't Dead featuring a tongue-in-cheek homage to his current stomping ground in the track, South Yorks.

After moving to The Steel City in the late 90s, Acne's first experience with Henderson's Relish occurred down at his local chippie. Drawing a sense of inspiration from Andy Warhol's Pop Art, he drew the original design in 2007 – making it one of the first Henderson's art homages. He believes that the success of the sauce can be put down to the way in which food brings people together, and, for the people of Sheffield, Henderson's Relish consistently unites families and friends at meal times. The key message behind the piece is simple, yet manages to encapsulate a small piece of the traditional Sheffield character, "eat well and be good to people." – not much to argue with there, eh? Those interesting characters around the bottle are ghosts; the idea being to incorporate a bit of northern 'spirit' into the piece. The boxing gloves are symbols of strength. Strong and Northern…tha knows.

www.kidacne.com

BEEF BURGER WITH
TOMATO KETCHUP

THIS MEATY BURGER AND SPICY TOMATO SAUCE WORK GREAT WITH HENDO'S.

INGREDIENTS

Henderson's tomato ketchup

1kg tomatoes, roughly chopped

½ onion, roughly diced

4 cloves garlic, chopped, green shoot removed

30g salt

300g white sugar

150ml red wine vinegar

50ml Henderson's Relish

½ tsp whole cloves

½ tsp chilli flakes

For the burgers

500g quality minced beef

1 large free-range egg, beaten

sea salt

Freshly ground black pepper

2 tbsp Henderson's Relish

2 tbsp fresh parsley, chopped

1 onion, fine diced and sautéed

For the buns

6 good-quality or fresh burger buns, halved

Olive oil

1 cos or round lettuce, washed & torn

3 tomatoes, sliced

1 red onion, sliced

3-4 gherkins, sliced

METHOD

For the ketchup

Put all ingredients in a pan and simmer for about 2 hours, stirring often to prevent burning.

Cool slightly then blend.

Sieve for a smooth sauce then store in sterilised kilner jars.

For the burgers

Mix all of the ingredients for the beef burgers together well, check for seasoning and shape into six patties.

Cook over a hot griddle for about 4 minutes on each side or to your liking.

Assemble the buns and serve with the spicy Henderson's ketchup.

GARY MANGHAM - THE WORTLEY ARMS

The Wortley Arms has been a cornerstone of this pretty village after which it was named for more than 250 years, but these days it's as well known for its food as it is for its history.

TRIPLE-DECKER
FRIED EGG SANDWICH

DAN WALKER IS A BROADCASTER AND JOURNALIST WHO STUDIED IN SHEFFIELD
AND HAS LIVED IN THE CITY WITH HIS FAMILY FOR YEARS.

INGREDIENTS

2-4 eggs (depending on hunger levels and manliness)

3 slices of thick white bread

Butter

Ketchup

Henderson's Relish

Knob butter

Vegetable oil

METHOD

Fry your eggs in a 70/30 mix of vegetable oil and butter. The butter stops the eggs from going too brown.

While the eggs are frying, butter two slices of bread. The third slice of bread is the key ingredient and is known as the relish wedge.

When the eggs are about 30 seconds off perfect, butter both sides of the relish wedge and put about 8 drops of relish on both sides.

Whip out the eggs and place 1-2 of the eggs on the the first slice and then add ketchup to taste.

Place on the relish wedge, then add the remaining fried eggs and then put the final slice on top.

If you want to go crazy, break a couple of the yokes so the yellow peril starts running down the sides of the bread.

Take a picture of your sandwich and spread it across social media with the hashtag #RelishWedge.

Nail sandwich perfection and devour with a cup of tea.

DAN WALKER - BROADCASTER & JOURNALIST

"I came to Sheffield as something of a Henderson's Relish neanderthal, unaware of the powers of the relish until I walked to my first ever lecture at Sheffield University. I remember smelling a wave of flavour as I strolled past the factory - like pickled onion monster munch but 72 times better. I started going out with a local lass - who is now my wife – and her family introduced me to Henderson's in spaghetti Bolognese, on meat pie and drizzled over cheese on toast. I have never looked back and have now introduced the power of the relish to many of my family and friends. This is the recipe that always does the business for me."

SWEDE & CELERIAC
PAKORAS

THE CHEFS AT HENDERSON'S OF EDINBURGH LOVE TO USE HENDERSON'S RELISH IN
THE KITCHEN. THIS RECIPE IS FOR THEIR SWEDE AND CELERIAC PAKORAS WITH A SPICY
HENDERSON'S RELISH DIP - AN INTERESTING AND TASTY WAY OF USING HENDO'S. MAKES 30

INGREDIENTS

For the Henderson's Relish dip

1 small onion

4 cloves garlic

15g fresh ginger

4 green Indian chillies

2 x 400g tins chopped tomatoes

2 dessert spoons garam masala

60ml Henderson's Relish

For the pakoras

80g swede

800g celeriac

600g gram flour

600ml sparkling water

1 dessert spoon chilli powder

1 dessert spoon cumin powder

1 dessert spoon coriander powder

2 dessert spoon cumin seed

*8 dessert spoons finely chopped fresh
coriander*

1½ dessert spoons ground sea salt

Oil for frying

METHOD

For the dip

Very finely dice the onion and garlic.

Peel and grate the ginger.

Finely slice the green chillies.

Combine all the ingredients together with the chopped tomatoes, garam
masala and Henderson's Relish and leave to stand for 30 minutes to
infuse the flavours.

For the pakoras

Finely dice the swede and celeriac.

In a separate dish, combine all the other ingredients to form a smooth
paste with the consistency of wet sand.

Now add the swede and celeriac and leave to stand at room temperature
for 20 minutes.

Fry in small batches in a deep fat fryer at 160°C for 4-5 minutes.

Check that they are cooked through and garnish with lemon wedges,
fresh coriander and serve with the Henderson's Relish dip.

HENDERSON'S OF EDINBURGH

Henderson's of Edinburgh was established in 1962 as Scotland's first vegetarian restaurant. It has continued for over 50 years with it's philosophy of serving fresh, healthy and organic, local food. We specialise in vegetarian, vegan and gluten free

We are proud to offer Henderson's Relish as a tasty accompaniment to compliment our hot dishes and salads. Customers often think that the Henderson's in Sheffield must be relations, though we are not, it does make for a talking point!

Shaun
DOANE

THERE MAY BE 'NO OVEN, NO PIE' - BUT WE ALL KNOW IT'S ABOUT THE HENDO'S.

Born in the old Jessop Hospital (a mere stone's throw away from the Henderson's factory) Shaun spent his youthful years in Beighton – where a bottle of Henderson's could always be found on the kitchen table. In true Sheffield fashion, Shaun worked in a steel mill for 12 years, after that he spent five years on the road with well-known local band, The Sharp Cuts.

However, Shaun is mostly renowned amongst Sheffielders for being the front man of The Everly Pregnant Brothers – Sheffield's favourite ukulele cover band. The Brothers formed as a dare after Pete Mckee, Richard Bailey, and Pete's son Charley McKee agreed to go on stage with their ukes during a Christmas party at the Forum in 2008.

Shaun joined a year later, and has seen the band go from strength to strength – selling out shows at iconic local venues such as Sheffield City Hall, The Lyceum Theatre, The Crucible Theatre and The Leadmill. Other notable feats include attracting an estimated crowd of 4,000 to The Fat Cat car park during Tramlines 2013 – going on to rock the Tramlines main stage the following day.

The Everly Pregnant Brothers' repertoire of Sheffield based covers includes their own versions of hits from acts such as Pulp, Bob Marley, Kings of Leon and The Clash. But it is the Henderson's inspired cover of Coldplay's Yellow which strikes a real chord with their audiences. During rehearsal, Shaun came up with the words pretty much on the spot, and in the space of half an hour, the verses were written and a musical ode to the relish was born.

STEAK & HENDERSON'S
PASTY

OUR RECIPE MAKES 4 MEDIUM SIZED PASTIES.
PREPARATION TIME: 30 MINUTES BAKING TIME: 35-45 MINUTES

INGREDIENTS

For the pastry

600g plain flour

150g chilled butter or margarine, cubed

150g chilled lard, cubed

100ml water

Good pinch of salt

For the filling

100ml Henderson's Relish

225g beef skirt or chuck steak, diced

1 medium onion, diced

100g swede, peeled and diced

100g potatoes, peeled and diced

Knob of Cornish butter

Freshly ground black pepper and salt to season

METHOD

Dice your beef and pour over the Henderson's Relish – mix and leave to marinate for a couple of hours or if time leave in the fridge overnight.

Preheat the oven to 180°C.

Make the pastry first, then while it's resting in the fridge prepare the rest of the ingredients.

For the pastry

Season the flour and sift into a large bowl. Add the lard and butter or margarine and using your fingers work into the flour until it forms the consistency of fine breadcrumbs.

Sprinkle with cold water, a tablespoon at a time and mix until a stiff dough is formed. Gently knead the dough on a floured work surface, then wrap in cling film and leave to rest in the fridge for 30 minutes.

For the filling

Peel and finely slice and chop the potatoes, onion and swede before mixing with your marinated beef & Henderson's relish mixture.

To assemble your pasties

Cut the pastry into four pieces and roll out each piece on a lightly floured surface. Each piece should be circular (20 to 25cm in diameter and between 3 and 4mm thick). Place a similar sized plate over the pastry and cut around for a neat circle, keeping the trimmings for your initials.

Divide the filling into 4 equal portions in the centre of each pastry circle, season and top with a small knob of butter.

Brush the edge of the pastry with water, fold one side over to make a half moon or D shape and crimp together between the forefinger and thumb of one hand and the forefinger of the other to create a seal along the side of the pastry.

Make initials from the pastry trimmings for whom the pasty is for and place on top of each pasty.

Place on a floured or lined pre-heated baking tray, brush with milk or beaten egg and bake for 35-45 minutes until the pastry is golden and brown and the filling cooked through.

Once baked take out of the oven and leave to cool slightly (15 minutes) before serving.

PROPER PASTY COMPANY

Living in seaside town of St Ives, John Worrall had a flash of inspiration while eating a steak and stilton Cornish pasty and gazing at the large queue forming outside the local pasty shop.

In 1999, he opened the first Proper Pasty Co. in his hometown of Sheffield – which has remained a firm favourite of local people looking for a tasty bite ever since.

ASHOKA
HOUSE PURI

HENDERSON'S RELISH IS INTRINSICALLY LINKED TO INDIA WITH IT'S EXOTIC FLAVOURS
DERIVED FROM TAMARIND, CAYENNE, GARLIC AND CLOVES. AT ASHOKA WE'VE
BEEN USING 'HENDOS' IN OUR HOUSE PURI FOR OVER THREE DECADES.

INGREDIENTS

For the filling

Large handful of baby potatoes

Salt to taste

3 cloves garlic finely chopped

¼ tsp chilli powder

¼ tsp turmeric powder

½ tsp curry powder

1 lemon

¼ can chickpeas

1 white onion, halved and thinly sliced

3-4 splashes Henderson's Relish

For the puri

4 dessert spoons plain flour

Water

½ tsp Salt

Vegetable oil for deep frying

Coriander leaves, to garnish

METHOD

First make the puri bread. Combine all the ingredients and make a dough, making sure to add the water slowly.

You're looking for a medium-firm dough. Cover with cling film and leave in the fridge to rest for 20 minutes.

Roll out a ping-pong sized ball of dough into a flat disc. Make sure you use plenty of flour on your rolling pin and board to avoid the dough sticking.

Heat the oil for frying. A great way to test the temperature is to fry a very small piece of the dough. If it sinks the oil isn't hot enough, if the dough stays at the surface and bubbles away the temperature is right.

Take the rolled puri bread and shake from hand-to-hand to remove excess flour and place in the oil away from you, to avoid being splashed with the hot oil.

Using a metal spatula as the puri is frying skim the surface of the oil and splash onto the puri as it rises. This does take some practice.

For the filling

Wash and cut the potato into approximately 1cm cubes.

Halve and thinly slice the onion.

In a large frying-pan, add 2 tablespoons of vegetable oil and gently bring to frying temperature.

Gently fry the potatoes and onions for a few minutes. Add the garlic, chilli powder, curry powder and turmeric and continue to cook on a medium heat for a further 10 minutes, stirring frequently to ensure the potatoes don't catch and burn.

Add the rinsed chickpeas, juice of half a lemon and Henderson's Relish. Taste and season with salt as required.

To serve, crack the top of the puri and place the filling inside.

Garnish with chopped coriander and serve.

ASHOKA RESTAURANT

Ashoka, named after the great Indian emperor, is a Sheffield institution; a cornerstone of Ecclesall Road since it was opened in 1967. Their successful formula is a simple one – fresh, high quality ingredients cooked by talented chef's and a long-standing front of house team.

CHEESE & BACON
MUFFINS

THIS SHOULD MAKE 9 MUFFINS.
PREPERATION TIME: 10 MINUTES. BAKING TIME: 20 MINUTES

INGREDIENTS

270g self-raising flour

130g strong Cheddar, grated (plus a little more for melting on top)

30g Parmesan, grated

½ tsp turmeric

½ tsp cayenne pepper

½ tsp mustard powder

½ tsp salt

½ tsp ground black pepper

4 rashers smoked bacon

1 small red onion

1 tsp fresh sage, chopped

100ml Greek yoghurt

100ml milk

2 eggs

60ml Henderson's Relish

Muffin cases or circles of greaseproof/silicone paper

METHOD

Preheat oven to 180°C.

Chop the onion into thin slices, chop the bacon into strips, fry on a medium heat together in olive oil for 5 minutes. Add the chopped sage and fry until the onions are starting to brown and the bacon fat is getting crispy.

Mix all the dry ingredients together.

Whisk together the eggs, yoghurt, milk and Henderson's Relish.

Mix this into the dry ingredients, then add the onion and bacon mix, making sure to incorporate all the ingredients, but being careful not to over mix.

If using circles of silicone paper, grease a muffin tin, then push the circles in to create a case.

Fill the mix to about half of the case, sprinkle with some extra Cheddar on top and bake for 15-20 minutes until the muffins are golden brown.

Once baked, take them out of the oven and let them rest in their cases on a cooling rack for 5 minutes before serving.

Tips:

To make it fiery, add a quarter of a teaspoon of ground ginger and double the amount of cayenne pepper.

DAVID STOUT

David is a keen hobbyist baker and enjoys experimenting with new flavour combinations in traditional bakes. He works for CODEC Research Centre at the University of Durham researching Theology and Digital Humanities. For a sweet breakfast muffin alternative, substitute the onion, sage, and half the yoghurt, for 50ml of maple syrup.

CHOCOLATE &
HENDO'S MOUSSE

HENDERSON'S RELISH IS A DIFFICULT ONE TO MATCH WITH A DESSERT,
BUT HAS AN AFFINITY WITH RICH CHOCOLATE.

INGREDIENTS

325g 70% dark chocolate

2 medium egg yolks

25g caster sugar

130ml milk

1 tsp Henderson's Relish

150ml whipping cream

400ml whipping cream

METHOD

Melt the chocolate slowly over gently simmering water or in a microwave.

Beat the egg yolks and sugar in a bowl until light in colour.

Heat the 150ml cream, milk and Henderson's Relish until a gentle simmer.

Slowly pour the cream onto the egg mixture, mixing continuously to avoid scrambling the eggs.

Pour back into a clean pan and stir.

Cook until the temperature reaches 80°C or the mixture coats the back of a spoon.

Remove from the heat, put into a cold bowl and immediately blend with a stick blender.

Pour onto the chocolate stirring continuously.

Whip the 400ml of cream into soft peaks.

When the chocolate mixture has cooled slightly fold in the whipped cream using a metal spoon or flat spatula

Pour into moulds or glasses as required and chill in the fridge.

LEN UNWIN - SHEFFIELD COLLEGE

As a Sheffield Master Chef and Chef Lecturer at Sheffield College, Len Unwin serves as mentor to aspiring young chefs learning their trade. Len has previously showcased his talents at Sheffield's Skills for Chefs conference – an event designed for leading chefs to share and pass on their culinary knowledge.

Lisa MALTBY

LISA'S HENDERSON'S EPIPHANY STARTED WITH A COTTAGE PIE.

Lisa Maltby first received her education in Henderson's Relish ten years ago, after she moved from Otley to Sheffield. To begin with, she couldn't help but wonder what all the fuss was about – however, a few Hendo's inspired cottage pies later and Lisa found herself well and truly converted.

The majority of Lisa's illustration work is based on her surroundings; Sheffield and its local culture have grown to become a key influence in some of her designs. For this particular piece, the aim was to create a retro-style advertisement which highlighted the traditional feel of the brand.

The image and typography were done by hand, whereas the colours and textures were added digitally – creating a contrasting style of the two. The illustration aims to capture the pride that Sheffielders feel in the old factory. Lisa believes that the building has a certain feel of authenticity which causes it to stand out amongst its modern counterparts – the huge orange sign helps, too!

www.lisamaltby.com

www.lisamaltby.com

TOMATO
CHILLI PICKLE

THE ACIDITY IN THE TOMATOES AND RELISH WORK WELL TOGETHER.
MAKES 12 JARS

INGREDIENTS

500g fresh tomatoes, chopped

250g tinned tomatoes, drained

2 red chillies, sliced

750g onions, chopped

400g granulated sugar

500ml malt vinegar

100ml Henderson's Relish

250g courgettes, diced

100g tomato purée

1 tbsp yellow mustard seeds

½ tbsp salt

500g apples, chopped

METHOD

Salt the courgettes overnight, rinse well and leave to drain.

Drain the tinned tomatoes.

Roughly chop the fresh tomatoes, onions and apples in a food processor, or by hand.

In a large saucepan, cook the onions with half of the vinegar on a medium heat for 10 minutes to soften the onions.

Add all the remaining ingredients, except the sugar, and cook for 20 minutes, stirring regularly.

When ingredients are softened, add sugar and cook for 30-45 minutes, stirring regularly so it does not stick to the pan.

It is ready when the chutney is thick enough to make a channel with your wooden spoon across the surface.

Have glass jars ready and sterilised, this can be done in an oven on 120°C for 20 minutes. Pot up whilst the chutney is hot and put lids on then leave to cool.

It will taste better after a few months in the jar!

MATT HULLEY - JUST PRESERVES

Despite a food marketing degree, and the conviction that his future lay in food, it took Just Preserves' owner Matt Hulley a while to hone his true calling.

A post-university customer services job in London didn't quite satisfy his appetite – so leaving the Big Smoke behind Matt pursued his calling and moved north to God's Own County.

Braised Beef Cheeks with
CRISPY FRIED OYSTERS

HENDERSON'S RELISH HAS INSPIRED THIS DISH FROM THE ISLAND OF GUERNSEY.
SERVES 4

INGREDIENTS

For the beef cheeks
4 beef cheeks
300g chopped shallots
300g wild mushrooms
200g bacon (cut into cubes or short strips)
30ml Henderson's Relish
750ml full bodied red wine
250ml dark ale
50g plain flour
20g fresh thyme
25ml vegetable oil
300g whole carrots, peeled
1 bay leaf
Salt and freshly ground black pepper
For the creamed potatoes
700g potatoes
50g butter
140ml fresh double cream
25g fresh thyme
For the crispy fried oysters
8 fresh oysters, shucked
2 egg yolks
2 egg whites
200g plain flour
150ml cold water
5ml Henderson's Relish
Oil for frying

METHOD

For the braised beef cheeks

Dredge each beef cheek with seasoned flour.

Add vegetable oil to a large frying pan and seal the beef cheeks until browned and caramelized. Remove then set aside.

Add the shallots and cubed bacon to the frying pan and cook until the onions have softened and the bacon has taken on a little colour.

Remove from the frying pan and place in a large casserole dish with the beef cheeks.

Add to this the carrots, picked thyme leaves and bay leaf.

Deglaze the frying pan with the ale and red wine.

Reduce slightly before adding to the casserole dish along with Henderson's Relish.

Cover the casserole dish with a tight fitting lid and place in oven for 3-3½ hours at 160°C.

After this time, add the wild mushrooms and braise for a further 20-30 minutes.

Check and adjust seasoning to taste.

For the creamed potatoes

Boil or steam the peeled potatoes until soft. Allow to drain before placing through a fine sieve.

Add the cream, butter and freshly picked thyme leaves. Mix until smooth and creamy.

Taste and adjust the seasoning prior to serving.

For the crispy fried oysters

In a bowl, beat the 2 egg yolks with the Henderson's Relish, cold water and sieved flour.

Set aside for around one hour to ferment the batter.

Before using, beat the egg whites to soft peaks and fold into the batter.

Dip the oysters into the batter and fry for 1 minute in hot oil.

Drain onto kitchen paper and serve.

the *Pavilion*

TONY LECK - THE PAVILION, GUERNSEY

Originally from Cumbria, Tony moved to Guernsey in 1987, where he worked as a young pastry chef. After widening his culinary knowledge through working at various dining establishments, Tony opened The Pavilion in 2000, which has since gone on to become the most highly regarded restaurant on the island.

The philosophy behind the The Pavilion is simple and effective: fresh, local produce cooked with little fuss.

Walnut & Seed
SALAD TOPPERS

A GREAT HEALTHY ALTERNATIVE TO PEP UP ANY SALAD DISH.

Ingredients

200g walnuts

100g pumpkin seeds

50g sunflower seeds

50g sesame seeds

50g black onion seeds

5 table brown sugar

2 tbsp water

2 tbsp Henderson's Relish

Method

Get a large heavy-bottomed pan and toast the nuts and seeds on a medium to high heat for about 3-5 minutes stirring continuously.

The pumpkin seeds should just begin to burst, a little like popcorn.

Add the sugar and water (be careful this may spit) then continue to stir as the water evaporates and the sugar sticks everything together for around 3 minutes.

Add the Henderson's Relish and stir some more until the seeds form large clusters.

Remove from the heat and spread onto a greaseproof lined baking tray to cool.

Keep in an air tight kilner jar.

These are super earthy flavoursome additions to any salad, adding a good source of protein to vegetarian dishes.

I've paired this with a fennel, radish, apple and watercress salad.

Jonty Cork - Made by Jonty

Since opening its doors in 2010, Made by Jonty has quickly become a much loved addition to the Sharrow Vale Road food scene. Jonty and his team pride themselves on providing high quality, locally sourced food for their customers in a friendly and relaxed environment.

Matt BREWIN

THE GENIUS OF LOCAL PHOTOGRAPHER MATT BREWIN IS EVIDENT IN THIS STUNNING PHOTOGRAPH OF HENDO'S.

What's going on here!? Shooting a bottle of Hendo's? Somebody needs to give their head a wobble!

Rest assured that photographer Matt Brewin loves his Henderson's just as much as the next Sheffielder – but every now and again Matt likes to show some tough love to an unfortunate member of his collection.

This striking image was captured in a photography studio, and getting the perfect shot was a complex process involving the use of use of laser beams, high speed camera flashes and, of course, an air rifle to fire at the bottle. Matt asked an assistant to shoot at the bottle; the pellet then broke through the laser beam triggering the flash lights and allowing the camera to capture an image of the bottle upon impact.

When asked whether he had a slightly guilty conscience afterwards, Matt claimed that he gained a strange sense of added respect for the relish after destroying a number of bottles. "The experience of working inside a studio pungent with the aroma of Hendo's, whilst studying every inch of the bottle design really causes you to become intermittent with the object. If you rub the sauce between your fingers, you notice minute flecks of orange and deep ruby hues – it's a beautiful thing."

CHOCOLATE PAVE WITH PINK PEPPERCORN
STRAWBERRIES

THE TANGY SWEETNESS OF HENDO'S COUPLED WITH RICH CHOCOLATE.

INGREDIENTS

200g unsalted butter

150ml Henderson's Relish

150g golden syrup

350g dark chocolate

Punnet of fresh English strawberries

10 pink peppercorns

Icing sugar to taste

To serve

Clotted cream ice cream

METHOD

In a pan melt the butter, golden syrup and Henderson's Relish.

Once fully melted, increase the heat and bring to the boil for 2 minutes. Remove from the heat and allow to cool for 1 minute, then add the chocolate.

Stir until smooth and melted. Pour in to a cling film tray and place in the fridge.

This will set firmly in a couple of hours.

Remove from the tray, cut into the desired shape and place on a serving plate allowing it to come back to room temperature.

In a bowl, quarter the strawberries and add the crushed peppercorns and a little icing sugar to taste.

Place in the fridge.

Plate the chocolate pave, add the strawberries and serve with clotted cream or ice cream.

CHARLIE CURRAN - PEPPERCORN

Peppercorn's head chef and co-owner Charlie Curran has over 25 years' experience. Working his way up the chef food chain in establishments like Headingley cricket ground and Leeds' Hayley's Hotel, Charlie's big career break came in the form of a role in Brian Turner's London restaurant where he eventually became head chef.

Five years later Sheffield beckoned Charlie back, where he realised the dream of running his own restaurant and bought Peppercorn.

BLACK BEAN &
SOYA BURGER

A SATISFYING BURGER THAT IS COMPLETELY MEAT FREE.

INGREDIENTS

For the burger relish
1 red onion, finely diced
1 red pepper, finely diced
1 garlic clove, crushed
100ml red wine vinegar
100ml Henderson's Relish
100g Demerara sugar
Salt and pepper
For the Henderson's rarebit
450g mature Cheddar, grated
60ml milk
1 garlic clove
30g plain flour
30g breadcrumbs
2 tsp English mustard
1 tsp paprika
1 tbsp parsley, chopped
1 tsp mustard powder
2 eggs, beaten
25ml Henderson's Relish
Salt and pepper
For the black bean and soya burger
250g dried soya mince
750ml water
1 onion, finely diced
1 tin pre-cooked black beans
50g cornflour
50g breadcrumbs
1 tbsp vegetable stock
1 tbsp parsley, chopped
2 tsp smoked paprika
1 tsp dried oregano
1tsp cayenne powder
1 tsp ground cumin
1 egg
Salt and pepper to taste

METHOD

For the burger relish

In a pan combine all the ingredients and slowly bring to a boil. Once boiling turn the heat down and leave it to simmer until reduced by half.

Remove from heat and leave to cool to room temperature.

Place everything in a blender and blend on the highest setting until well mixed. Pass the contents through a fine sieve and push through with a metal spoon.

Taste the relish and adjust seasoning if needed. If the relish is a little runny return to a pan and reduce to the required consistency.

For the rarebit

It is best to have everything prepared before you start cooking.

In a large heavy-bottomed pan put the grated cheese, garlic and milk.

In a small bowl combine the flour, breadcrumbs, mustard powder, paprika, salt and pepper.

In another bowl beat the eggs, Henderson's Relish and English mustard.

Line a flat baking tray with a sheet of greaseproof paper, and cut another sheet the same size.

Place the pan over a low heat and start to melt the cheese. Use a heat proof spatula to keep stirring the mix so it doesn't stick or burn.

Once the cheese is melted and is easy to stir, remove from the heat and quickly beat in the egg mixture. Keep mixing until it's fully combined.

Next beat the dry flour mixture in and mix well.

Tip the contents of the pan out onto the greaseproof tray. Place the other sheet on top and using a rolling pin push the mixture out until it covers the tray and is about 5mm deep.

Place in the fridge and leave until needed.

For the burger

Finely dice the onion and sauté for 10 minutes until translucent. Be careful they don't burn or stick. Remove from the heat and leave to cool.

In a separate pan bring the water, spices, veg stock and dried herbs to a boil. Once boiling add the dried soya mince, mix thoroughly and leave to cool.

Once cooled in a large bowl combine all the ingredients and mix thoroughly with your hands. Leave to rest for 30 minutes.

After resting, shape the burgers to your required size and leave in the fridge until needed.

To assemble the burger

Add a splash of oil to a frying pan then fry your burger until it is nicely coloured on both sides. Transfer to a medium oven for 7 minutes at 160°C.

While the burger is cooking the rarebit needs portioning. Remove from the fridge and slide onto a chopping board and cut to a size that will fit on top of the burger.

Remove the greaseproof paper and place on the burger and then grill for 2 minutes until the rarebit looks crispy but not burnt.

Use the relish on the bun and add whatever takes your fancy.

JON TITE - THE SHOWROOM

The Sous Chef of the Showroom kitchen, Jon specialises in vegetarian dishes. Originally starting as bar manager, he later entered the kitchen and flourished after being trained on the job. In 2013 and 2014, he reached the final of the Vegetarian Society's Chef of the Year award.

VEGETARIAN
SHEPHERD'S PIE

THIS IS A HEARTY VEGETARIAN ALTERNATIVE TO A TRADITIONAL SHEPHERD'S PIE.
SERVES 4-6

INGREDIENTS

1 tbsp olive oil

2 garlic cloves

1 large onion, or 2 sticks celery

2 large carrots

2 tbsp chopped fresh thyme

5 tbsp Henderson's Relish

200ml red wine

400g chopped tomatoes

200g pearl barley, or red lentils

2 tbsp marmite

1kg sweet potatoes, roasted

2 tbsp butter

Grated vegetarian cheese, optional

METHOD

In a frying pan, heat the olive oil.

Slice the garlic and dice the vegetables then fry until lightly brown.

Add the thyme, red wine, Henderson's Relish and marmite and cook for 2 minutes.

Add the tomatoes and pearl barley and cook for 20 minutes.

Add the mixture to an ovenproof dish.

Mash the roasted sweet potatoes with the butter and add to the top of the mixture.

Add the cheese to the top if desired.

Place under the grill until the top is crispy and golden.

NICK WILKES - ST LUKES HOSPICE

Founded in 1971, St Luke's Hospice delivers expert care to patients with incurable illnesses – providing the best quality of life available and support for family, friends and carers. Each year, the hospice supports more than 1,400 people with a terminal illness. In March 2013, St Luke's teamed-up with Henderson's Relish for the "Great Pie and Peas Up" to help raise funds needed to build a new inpatient unit for the hospice.

Sam BAJDALA-CRESSEY

RECOGNISED FOR THE STRONG AND SIMPLE DESIGN, ARTWORK FROM SAM
GRACES THE WALLS OF MANY SHEFFIELD BUILDINGS – INCLUDING OUR OFFICE!

As a local Sheffield lad, Sam Bajdala-Cressey was educated at Norton College and Hallam University. After graduating with a degree in graphic design, Sam invested time into travelling and gaining valuable experience as a graphic designer. He has now set up NL Wall Art where he uses his design talents to create posters and wall décor.

Sam likes to describe his style as minimal; the aim is to create an end product which is simplistic, yet effective at getting the message of the piece across. Some of his earliest memories include the familiar sight of a Henderson's Relish bottle which stood constantly on the table of his grandparents' house. He describes the taste of Henderson's as a "warm blanket" which makes him feel at home.

'Undiscovered Sauce' is one piece from a set of four Henderson's inspired pieces from the artist. It aims to celebrate the uniqueness of the sauce, which his friends would take to various universities to share with colleagues from across the UK in an effort to spread the word of the relish.

www.nlwallart.co.uk

**YET TO BE DISCOVERED
IN ANY OTHER TOWN OR CITY**

THE LAUNDRETTE
BLOODY MARYS

HERE AT THE LAUNDRETTE WE ARE PROUD USERS OF HENDERSON'S RELISH, NOT ONLY ON THE BAR - IN OUR SEVEN 'BLOODY GOOD' MARYS - BUT ALSO IN THE KITCHEN IN OUR FAMOUS BURGERS AND FIERY KETCHUP.

THE LAUNDRETTE MARY

INGREDIENTS

50ml citrus vodka

20ml fresh lemon juice

5ml sugar syrup

100ml tomato juice

25ml Henderson's Relish

Pinch of salt

Pinch of pepper

¼ tsp paprika

½ tsp horseradish sauce

2 dashes celery bitters

5ml white wine vinegar

Tabasco (as hot as you dare!)

Stick celery

Sliced gherkins

METHOD

Stir all of the ingredients together in a glass and pour over ice.

Serve with a stick of celery, gherkin slice and a straw.

THE FILTHY SWINE

INGREDIENTS

50ml bacon infused vodka

10ml lemon juice

5ml sugar syrup

100ml tomato juice

25ml Henderson's Relish

15ml brown sauce

pinch of salt

pinch of pepper

5ml white wine vinegar

Tabasco (as hot as you dare!)

Stick celery

Sliced gherkins

Rasher grilled bacon

METHOD

Stir all of the ingredients together in a glass and pour over ice.

Serve with a stick of celery, gherkin slice, rasher of hot bacon and a straw.

THE LAUNDRETTE, MANCHESTER

We are a small, independent restaurant and bar, dedicated to providing delicious food, amazing cocktails and a relaxing and friendly atmosphere – be it for a cosy winter's evening, or a sunny afternoon on the terrace.

HENDERSON'S & BLACK TREACLE
CURED SALMON

THIS IS A VERSION OF GRAVLAX. INSTEAD OF DILL WE USE HENDERSON'S RELISH
AND BLACK TREACLE TO CURE THE SALMON.

INGREDIENTS

For the dry cure
1kg organic salmon fillet, skinned
60g caster sugar
40g Maldon sea salt
1 star anise
5 peppercorns
For the wet cure
200ml Henderson's Relish
330g black treacle
100g caster sugar
1 lemon, juiced
1 lime, juiced
1 orange, juiced
For the garnish
1 loaf rye bread
1 lemon

JUSTIN BROWN

Winner of Pub Chef of the Year award three years on the trot, Justin Brown is one of the country's most talented up and coming chefs. He's packed an enormous amount into his career already, including working for Jamie Oliver and Rolling Stones' Ronnie Wood as well as cooking for Andrew Lloyd Webber, David Beckham and Madonna.

METHOD

For the dry cure

This dish requires the freshest salmon you can get. Remove the skin from the salmon and any pin bones.

Mix the caster sugar, sea salt, star anise and peppercorns together in a bowl.

Dry the salmon with a cloth and place half the salt/sugar mixture on a baking tray

Lay the salmon on top then cover with the remaining mix. Leave to cure for 5 hours.

Once cured remove the salmon and wash under cold water to remove all the sugar/salt mixture. This will start the curing process by removing some of the moisture from the salmon.

For the wet cure

Mix the Henderson's Relish, black treacle, caster sugar, lemon, lime and orange juice in a bowl with a whisk.

Once mixed, place the salmon side in a deep container and pour over the wet cure, covering the fish.

Leave covered up in the fridge for 2 days turning the fish in the cure every 12 hours.

When cured the outside flesh will have taken on the colour and flavour from the Henderson's Relish but when you slice into the fish it will retain that bright orange colour of the salmon.

Once cured, remove the fish and pat off any excess cure. Discard the cure and refrigerate the fish until needed.

To serve, slice the salmon at an angle, as thinly as possible.

Place 5-6 thin slices of the salmon on each plate then serve with a wedge of lemon, a few slices of rye bread and garnish with micro-herbs.

BLUE CHEESE MOUSSE WITH
LORD MARPLES BREAD

CHEESE ON TOAST HAS ALWAYS BEEN A HENDO'S FAVOURITE.
THIS DISH REALLY SHOWS HOW CREATIVE CHEFS CAN BE.

INGREDIENTS

For the Lord Marples bread

250g white bread flour

250g malted grain flour

1 pint Thornbridge Brewery Lord Marples, reduced (reduce a pint by boiling until only 300ml remain, allow to cool to room temperature)

1 tsp lemon thyme leaves

10g fresh yeast

5g salt

For the Henderson's Relish jelly

270ml roast chicken stock, or vegetable stock if you prefer

30ml Henderson's Relish

3 gelatine leaves, or 3g of agar agar

Harrogate Blue mousse

200g Shepherd's Purse Harrogate Blue cheese

80ml creme fraîche

1 tsp chives, finely chopped

1 tsp pickled shallots, finely diced

For the onion ash

1 onion, sliced

METHOD

For the onion ash, start this a day in advance.

Cut the onion into thin slices and dry fry in a pan or over a BBQ.

When blackened and charred, dry in a warm place such as a low temperature oven at approximately 60°C, to dehydrate completely.

Blitz in food processor until the onion is dust then store in an airtight container

For the bread

Combine all the ingredients in a bowl, mix together then knead for 10 minutes until the dough is smooth.

Leave in the bowl and cover with cling film or a damp tea towel for a couple of hours or until the dough has risen (proved) and doubled in size.

Remove from the bowl and knead the dough again for only a minute.

Prepare your baking tin (a loaf tin or square cake tin will be fine) by brushing a little soft butter inside and sprinkling the inside surface with a little flour, shape the dough so it fits the tin.

Heat the oven to 220°C. Leave the dough in a warm place for 30 minutes to rise again to about double its size.

When this has happened, place the tin in the oven, throw in a splash of water to create a little steam and bake for 15-20 minutes, depending on the size of the tin.

For the Henderson's Relish jelly

Prepare a flat tray by making sure it's clean and dry then wipe a little cooking oil on the tray.

Soak the gelatine leaves in cold water until they soften.

Heat the stock and Henderson's Relish in a pan.

Squeeze the gelatine leaves to remove any excess water into the stock with a spatula.

Sieve the mix into a jug, check the flavour, it may need a little salt or another splash or two of Henderson's depending on the stock and your own taste.

Now pour the mix onto the greased tray. It needs to be quite thin, no more than 2mm.

Place in the fridge to set, making certain the tray is flat or the jelly won't set flat.

For the mousse

Finely dice a shallot, add it to a dry saucepan on a medium heat and add a dessert spoon of white wine vinegar, as soon as the vinegar has boiled away remove from the heat and allow to cool.

Now put the cheese and creme fraîche in a food processor (you can use a bowl and whisk if you're feeling energetic) beat the mix until smooth then add the chopped chives and shallot and place in a piping bag.

To assemble the dish, cut squares of the jelly and pipe the cheese mousse down one side of the square, roll the mousse and jelly so the mouse is wrapped in the jelly.

Cut thick soldiers of the bread and toast under the grill or in the toaster.

Sprinkle the onion ash on the plate (this will give the dish a bitter sweet roasted flavour).

Place the toast on the onion ash then the mousse and jelly on the toast.

Finally garnish with some thin slices of raw radish, more pickled shallots, and a few leaves; I've used red mustard and celery shoots here.

DARREN GOODWIN - LOSEHILL HOUSE HOTEL

Losehill House is the only four star hotel in the Peak District National Park.

Head chef Darren Goodwin's passion is fine dining and his daily changing menus mean the food is constantly evolving. Dishes are created from what's seasonally available at market, meaning absolute freshness with plenty of creative flair and eye-catching, precise presentation.

Katey FELTON

POSH UP YOUR HENDERSON'S WITH A BIT OF BLING.

Originally from Skegness in Lincolnshire, Katey Felton moved to Sheffield in 2001 where she completed a two year starter programme in silversmithing. She now runs a successful silversmiths business based in the Persistence Works building – a part of Sheffield's Yorkshire Artspace.

The inspiration for her design came whilst dining with a friend on the traditional Yorkshire delicacy of pie, chips and mushy peas (or should that be peys?) Katey decided that she would like to adorn her trusty bottle of Henderson's with silver, which would provide the brand with the touch of class it deserved. Also significant to Katey's design was the symbolism of joining two great Sheffield traditions, metalwork and Henderson's Relish.

As you can imagine, the limited edition silverware went down a treat and was purchased by Hendo's lovers to celebrate birthdays, weddings, anniversaries or simply to have their own glamorous bottle kept away in the cupboard for special occasions. The original product was proudly presented to previous owner, Dr Freeman. Since then, she has received shipping orders from all around the world.

www.kateyfelton.com

Ox Tail
COTTAGE PIE

IN OUR VERSION OF COTTAGE PIE WE USE RICH OX TAIL FOR A TOUCH OF LUXURY

Ingredients

1.5kg ox tail

2 onions, finely chopped

2 garlic cloves, finely chopped

3 carrots, finely chopped

3 celery sticks, chopped

1 tbsp tomato purée

3 tbsp plain flour

250ml red wine

850ml beef stock

4 tbsp Henderson's Relish

2 sprigs thyme

2 bay leaves

Oil for frying

Salt & pepper

For the mashed potato

2kg potatoes chopped

225ml milk

25g butter

200g strong chedder cheese, grated

Nutmeg, grated

Method

Place the ox tail into a pressure cooker and fill with water.

Leave it to cook out for 45 minutes, once it is are done leave to cool down and shred by hand, keeping all the juices and water aside as this can be used for the stock.

Place all the vegtables into a pan with a little oil and cook for around 20 minutes until soft.

Add the garlic, flour and tomato purée, then increase the heat and cook for a few minutes.

Place all the meat into the pan with your vegetables and pour over the red wine. Boil to reduce down a little before adding the beef stock, Henderson's Relish and herbs then bring to a simmer and cook uncovered for 45 minutes.

By this time the gravy should be thick and coating the meat. Remove the bay leaves and thyme stalks then season well.

Meanwhile, make the mashed potato in a large saucepan. Cover the potaoes in cold salted water and bring to the boil, simmer until tender

Drain well then allow to steam-dry for a few minutes.

Mash well with milk, butter and three quarters of the cheese, then season to taste with salt, pepper and grated nutmeg.

Spoon the meat into an ovenproof dish and pipe or spoon the mash on top to cover all the meat. Sprinkle on the remaining cheese if eating straight away.

Heat the oven to 220°C and cook for 30 minutes until the topping is golden.

Eat with your favourite seasonal vegetables, my choice would be baby carrots, cabbage and broccoli with a large serving of gravy – not forgetting the main star of the show, Henderson's Relish.

DEVONSHIRE ARMS MIDDLE HANDLEY

Situated in the small Derbyshire village of Middle Handley, The Devonshire Arms is a family-owned gastropub which takes great pride in the serving of quality food, excellent ales and fine wines. This year saw the hard work pay off as it entered the 2014 Michelin Guide to Pubs and Restaurants and the Telegraph's 500 Best Restaurants list respectively.

CORNED BEEF HASH POTATO CAKE WITH SOFT POACHED EGG

COMFORT FOOD IS THE IDEAL PARTNER FOR HENDERSON'S RELISH.
SERVES 4 (STARTER SIZE PORTIONS)

INGREDIENTS

For the corned beef hash potato cake

1 good quality tin of corned beef (At Rudding Park we make our own slow cooked corned beef but if you buy a good quality product this is also tasty)

½kg potatoes, washed & peeled

20g salted butter

20g gherkins, drained & chopped

2 tbsp Yorkshire rapeseed oil

1 small white onion peeled, finely chopped

2 tbsp Henderson's Relish

2 tbsp chopped, fresh herbs for the corned beef hash cake (we are using parsley and chives)

2 tbsp fresh herbs for the herb breadcrumbs, chopped

4 eggs, for poaching

1 tsp white wine vinegar

3 eggs, for coating the potato cakes

100g plain flour, seasoned with salt and pepper

100g bread crumbs

Your favourite mix of salad leaves

1 fresh lemon

2 tbsp Yorkshire rapeseed oil

Rock salt flakes and pepper

METHOD

Bring the peeled potatoes to the boil in salted water. Once boiling, reduce the heat to a simmer and cook until soft. This usually takes around 15-20 minutes. Drain the water and place the pan back on the heat to dry off any excess moisture for a few moments. Take the pan off the heat, mash the potatoes and add the salted butter. Don't forget to taste the mash!

Pan fry the chopped white onions with 2 tablespoons of Yorkshire rapeseed oil. Add the Henderson's Relish, diced corned beef and gherkins. Remove from the heat and add to the mash potato. Once cooled, add the chopped fresh herbs, correct the seasoning and fashion the mash into 4 cakes.

Place each cake into the seasoned flour and dust well. Whisk 3 eggs, coat the cakes in egg wash. Blend the breadcrumbs with 2 tablespoons of chopped herbs in a food processor for a few seconds and the crumbs will turn a very attractive bright green colour. Dip the cakes into the crumb mixture making sure they have a good all over coating. Place the cakes into a frying pan on a medium heat and pan fry in the rapeseed oil, turning regularly, until hot inside and crispy on the outside with a golden colour.

Dress your salad leaves with a drizzle of oil and a squeeze of fresh lemon juice and place on the plate.

To poach the eggs make sure the eggs are very fresh and free range. Season some boiling water with rock salt flakes and add one teaspoon of white wine vinegar. Crack the eggs carefully into 4 cups. Make a whirlpool vortex in the pan with a wooden spoon and gently place the eggs in the pan and simmer. After a few minutes the eggs will be perfectly poached and ready to place on top of the cake to serve.

The egg will ooze the perfectly cooked yolk over the Henderson's corned beef hash cake.

STEPHANIE MOON

Stephanie is a recognised figure on the Yorkshire food scene and has many accolades to her name including Yorkshire Life magazine 'Chef of the Year', Deliciously Yorkshire Champion, and a Bronze medal in the National 2010 British Culinary Federation 'Chef of the Year' Competition.

HENDERSON'S CHOCOLATE TRUFFLES

THIS IS A GREAT WAY TO SPOIL YOUR GUESTS.

INGREDIENTS

87g whipping cream

37g full fat milk

37g butter

250g plain dark chocolate 60-70% cocoa butter content

15ml Henderson's Relish

Cocoa powder used for rolling the truffles

150g plain dark chocolate 60-70% cocoa butter for rolling the truffles

METHOD

Boil the cream, milk and butter.

Melt the chocolate in a bowl over a pan of simmering water and gradually add the boiled cream mixture.

Finish using a stick blender to achieve a smooth and shiny mixture. Add the Henderson's Relish. This mixture is known as a ganache.

Pour into a tray and leave in a cool area until the ganache is firmly set.

Taking a tablespoon scrape up 15g pieces of the set ganache.

Shape round using your hands dipped in cocoa powder. This will prevent the ganache from sticking to your hands whilst processing.

To finish the truffles melt the 150g of plain chocolate in a bowl over a pan of simmering water.

Pour the melted chocolate onto a sheet of tin foil and dip one hand into the chocolate.

Take a shaped truffle and roll between both hands until a thin even coating is obtained.

Before the chocolate coating sets roll in cocoa powder giving an even coating.

MICK BURKE - SHEFFIELD COLLEGE

As Senior Chef Lecturer at The Sheffield College, Mick Burke is tasked with bringing through the next generation of local chefs to continue the city's proud food heritage. In 2013, Mick's service to the catering industry was recognised as he was made a Fellow of the Master Chefs of Great Britain for his continued work with young chefs in the city.

Matt COCKAYNE

THE OLD HENDERSON'S RELISH FACTORY HAS INSPIRED SEVERAL PIECES OF ART

Originally from Halfway, Matt Cockayne left Aston Comprehensive in 2000 and studied a graphics and sign writing BTEC at Castle College. After leaving college, Matt went through a number of jobs as he pursued his dream of becoming a graphic designer. He found a job as an artwork assistant with Crown Products; it was there he developed his design skills over the space of a four year employment. After being unable to afford a piece of artwork for his home, Matt decided, in true Sheffield fashion, to get the job done himself and create his own design. First of all, he created 'Captain Hendo' and followed up with an artwork series called 'Attack of the Hendo's' – featuring drops of Henderson's smashing into various Sheffield landmarks (God forbid!).

He launched his own label, 'Goo Design', and has worked closely with Henderson's to produce his own limited edition bottle design which commemorated his 'Working Class Heroes' exhibition. Matt chose to feature the Henderson's Relish factory in print due to its iconic status and its need to be celebrated in every way possible. Growing up, he was told by his father that the relish would "put hairs on thee chest!" – Something which Matt obviously took to heart as he now splashes it liberally over his 'meat and tatty' pies. When asked the age old question of what goes on inside the factory, he mentions his personal theory: "I think it could be Willy Wonka and the DeeDars inside there!"

goo-design.myshopify.com

TROJAN BOSS
BEEF STEW

NOTHING WARMS UP THE WINTER BLUES BETTER THAN A BIG BOWL OF STEW.

INGREDIENTS

600g beef stewing steak

2 tbsp plain flour

1 clove of garlic, crushed

175g onions, diced

150g celery, diced

150g carrots, diced

200g swede, diced

330ml Guinness Export

440ml Red Stripe

500ml beef stock

1 Scotch bonnet pepper, diced

2 fresh bay leaves

1 spring parsley

1 sprig thyme

Oil for frying

Salt and ground black pepper

30ml Henderson's Relish

For the dumplings

125g plain flour, plus extra for dusting

1 tsp baking powder

60g suet

Salt and ground black pepper

Water, to make the dough

METHOD

Preheat the oven to 160°C

Dice the onion, celery, carrots and swede into chunks.

Add a little oil to your casserole dish and brown the vegetables. Once browned remove from the pan.

Next toss your meat in the flour and add to the pan to brown, then add the vegetables back to the pan.

Add the aromatics, these being the pepper, bay leaves, parsley, garlic and thyme.

Next add the beers and the beef stock and stir well to combine all the ingredients.

Season generously with black pepper and a good glug of Henderson's Relish.

Bring to the boil, place a lid on top, then cook for 3-4 hours in the oven until tender.

Serve with mashed potato and, of course, more Henderson's Relish!

For the dumplings

Combine all the dry ingredients.

Make a well in the middle and add the water to make a dough.

To cook place golf-ball sized dumplings in your stew for the last hour of cooking to make them fluffy and juicy.

David Hancock - Trojan Explosion

Tasked with bringing the original sounds of ska, reggae, rocksteady and R&B to Sheffield, Dave Hancock can often be found behind the SFL Soundsystem decks, shaking the dance floor at The Riverside Bar and Café in Neepsend. With a large following of admirers, including Pete McKee and Richard Hawley, Trojan Explosion has quickly established itself as Sheffield's premier Jamaican ska and boss sounds event.

NICK CLEGG'S
PASTA BAKE

NOT ONLY IS THIS A VERY TASTY DISH THAT BRINGS OUT THE VERY BEST IN HENDERSON'S, IT IS ALSO (FOR SOMEONE AS POOR IN THE KITCHEN AS I AM) A STRAIGHTFORWARD MEAL TO COOK. THE PERFECT WINTER DINNER FOR PARENTS TO COOK FOR THEMSELVES AND (IN MY EXPERIENCE) THREE HUNGRY BOYS!

INGREDIENTS

1 tbsp olive oil

1 onion, diced

1 large carrot, diced

1 stick celery, diced

250g pork mince

250g beef mince

1 garlic clove, crushed

2x400g tins chopped tomatoes

2 tbsp tomato purée

350g penne pasta

100g Cheddar cheese, grated

450ml milk

25g flour

25g butter

Henderson's Relish

METHOD

Warm the oil in a pan and add the onion, carrot and celery – cook for 5 minutes. Increase the heat and add the mince and garlic and fry for a short while. Add a decent splash of Henderson's Relish to the mixture and give it a mix.

Add the tomatoes and tomato purée and cook for 5 minutes. Season with another splash of Henderson's Relish. Let it cook for around another 20 minutes.

Whilst the Henderson's medley is cooking away, prepare the white sauce. Heat the butter in a large pan until melted and then stir in the flour and cook for a minute. Whisk in the milk and bring to the boil letting the sauce thicken. Stir in half the Cheddar to taste.

Cook the pasta until just tender.

Preheat the oven to 200°C. Spread the meat in a deep gratin dish, add the pasta to the top of this and then the cheese sauce on top. Sprinkle with more Cheddar and scatter a sprinkling of Henderson's on the top. This will come up as lovely, crispy Henderson's infused cheese.

If you want to do this as a vegetarian dish – just replace the mince with veggies.

NICK CLEGG - DEPUTY PRIME MINISTER

The Deputy Prime Minister and leader of the Liberal Democrats has been MP for Sheffield Hallam since 2005. Born and raised in the Buckinghamshire village of Chalfont St Giles, he went on to study at the University of Cambridge, the University of Minnesota and the College of Europe in Bruges. In 1999, he was elected as the Liberal Democrat MEP for the East Midlands. After standing down from his MEP role in 2004, he won the constituency seat for Sheffield Hallam during the 2005 general election with over 50% of the vote.

LUKE FRENCH - THE MILESTONE

The future of this much-loved gem in Kelham Island's culinary crown was very nearly jeopardised by the floods of 2007 – just six months after opening.

From early foundations as a sports bar, serving up pizza and tapas, The Milestone has evolved into a gastro pub with culinary flare – boosted by the acclaim of being named Gordon Ramsay's Best British Restaurant in 2010.

The Milestone team has since honed its identity to become a Sheffield favourite with strong, gutsy food, local sourcing and nose-to-tail cooking using every part of the animal – an education for staff and diners alike.

CHEESE ON TOAST
TOAST ON CHEESE

HENDERSON'S RELISH, LARDO, WHIPPED YORKSHIRE GOATS' CURD
& FRESH GARDEN SHOOTS

INGREDIENTS

For the cheese toast

250g Parmesan

250g mature Cheddar

500g rolled oats

30ml white truffle oil

20g Maldon sea salt

For the Henderson's Relish gel

284ml Henderson's Relish

8 leaves gelatine

4.5g agar agar

Water

For the Lardo

A piece of good quality Lardeaux Di Colonatta (Lardo)

(Continued on page 116)

METHOD

For the cheese toast, finely grate the cheeses and combine.

Toast the oats in a dry pan and mix thoroughly with the grated cheeses, oil and salt.

Spread evenly on to a baking sheet lined with silicone paper and bake in the oven at 180°C for 15 minutes.

Remove and place on a cooling rack to cool. Break into toast like pieces and reserve in an airtight container until needed.

For the Henderson's Relish gel

Place the gelatine in cold water for 5-10 minutes until soft.

Place the Henderson's Relish in to a measuring jug and top it up with cold water to 625ml.

Pour the diluted Henderson's into a pan and slowly heat to boiling point, gradually begin to whisk in the agar agar and continue to whisk thoroughly over a high heat for 3 minutes whilst boiling.

Remove from the heat and set aside.

Squeeze out any water from the gelatine and gradually stir it into the hot liquid.

Pass through a fine sieve lined with muslin and leave to set in the fridge.

When set, place it in a food processor and blend on high speed until a smooth purée, then pass through a fine sieve once more. Reserve in the fridge until needed.

For the smoked lardo

It is not essential that the Lardo is smoked but it adds a great depth of flavour to the dish, if you have a smoking gun or smoker, then perfect!

Make sure the lardo is very well chilled before preparing to smoke it.

Cut the lardo in to small cubes and place in a roasting tin lined with silicone paper.

Place some smoking chips in to the smoking gun, then place the end of the pipe into the tin. Holding the pipe in place, tightly wrap it all the way around using cling film to make sure no smoke will escape.

Turn the smoking gun on and carefully burn the smoking chips using a blowtorch, when the tin is completely filled with smoke, turn off the gun and remove the pipe from the tin, making sure to quickly seal the hole tightly with more cling film so that no smoke is able to escape.

Place the tin in the fridge and leave it until all the smoke has disappeared.

Transfer the smoked lardo to a suitable container and reserve in the fridge until needed. (Continued on page 108)

CHEESE ON TOAST
TOAST ON CHEESE

INGREDIENTS

For the pumpkin seeds

10ml vegetable oil

50g pumpkin seeds

Maldon sea salt

For the crispy shallots

1 banana shallot

Gram flour to coat

Oil for deep frying

Maldon sea salt

For the whipped goat's curd

500g Yorkshire goat's curd

50g mascarpone

25ml double cream

5ml white truffle oil

Salt

White pepper

METHOD

For the pumpkin seeds; heat the oil in a small pan then add the pumpkin seeds and cook until they have all popped open and have turned golden in colour.

Remove from the heat and season with Maldon sea salt and cool completely. Reserve in an airtight container until needed.

For the crispy shallots; peel the shallot and slice into 2mm thickness using a mandolin.

Toss the shallot rings in enough gram flour just to coat them and then deep fry in oil at 170°C until golden and crispy, remove from the oil and toss in some kitchen paper.

Season with Maldon sea salt.

Reserve in an airtight container until needed.

For the whipped goat's curd; Place the curd and mascarpone in a food processor and gradually drizzle the cream in, followed by the truffle oil.

Blend the mixture until it becomes light and smooth and slightly aerated.

Season with salt and pepper to taste.

Remove the mix from the food processor and reserve in a piping bag placed in the fridge until needed.

To serve; Remove the curd from the fridge 10 minutes before serving.

Carefully pipe some quiffs of the curd on to a nice natural, rustic looking plate.

Place some pieces of the cheese toast on top of the curd, then pipe some smaller quiffs of curd on top of the cheese toast.

Arrange some pieces of the smoked lardo on and around the cheese toasts and then squeeze a good helping of the Henderson's Relish fluid gel on top.

Scatter some of the toasted pumpkin seeds over the dish.

Allium shoots such as leek, spring onion or garlic go very well with this dish.

Toss them in a little extra virgin olive oil, a drop of aged white balsamic vinegar and a pinch of sea salt and then scatter them all over, letting them fall naturally over the plate.

Finely grate some good quality aged Parmesan all over the dish, then drop the crispy shallot rings over the top.

Jim
CONNOLLY

COMICSTRIPS FROM JIM CONNOLLY ARE AS LEGENDARY AS THE SAUCE.

Jim Connolly grew up in the Steel City, but it took him over twenty years to succumb to the saucy powers of Henderson's Relish through the persuasion of friends. After studying Illustration & Animation at Manchester Metropolitan University, Jim returned to Sheffield and began to develop his talent for comic-style art – working on side-projects such as gig posters, CD covers and t-shirt designs. Inspired by the way artists such as Pete McKee and Kid Acne used artwork to put their own stamp on the Henderson's brand, Jim saw an opportunity to create his own slant on the sauce.

Use the Sauce features 'Hendo's girl', who uses her impressive kinetic powers to add a few drops of relish to her tea. The artist strived to give the girl an air of Sheffield – so you could imagine her partying at a Pulp gig or batting eyelashes at the Arctic Monkeys on Division Street.

Jim describes Henderson's Relish as a 'classic brand that doesn't try too hard.' He says it has become a rite of passage for Sheffielders...especially when partnered with steak & ale pie!

www.jimcportfolio.co.uk

BLOODY MARY &
CRAB CANNELLONI

ONE FOR THE CHEFS FROM MICHELIN-STARRED RESTAURANT, FISCHER'S OF BASLOW.
THEY SHOWCASE HENDERSON'S RELISH IN THIS IMAGINATIVE DISH.

INGREDIENTS

For the bloody Mary
375ml tomato juice
5 squirts Tabasco
50ml ruby Port
100ml vodka
3 turns of pepper
2 pinches celery salt
½ lime juice
50ml Henderson's Relish
For a more cheffy take;
0.9g gellan gum LT100 (MSK Brand)
0.9g gellan gum type F (MSK Brand)
5g caster sugar
500ml bloody Mary
For the crab ice cream
450g brown crab meat
1 tsp tomato paste
2tsp Armagnac
1130ml milk
400ml whipping cream
470g maltodextrin
8g salt
2 squirts tabasco
30ml Henderson's Relish
½ lime juice
For the Henderson's Relish purée
1 bottle Henderson's Relish
Ultratex (MSK brand)
For the crab
400g picked white crabmeat
75g crème fraiche
Fresh coriander
Salt
Lemon juice
For the pickled cucumber
300g white wine vinegar
150ml water
80g sugar
1g peppercorns
1g caraway seeds
1 cucumber

METHOD

For the bloody Mary; Mix all the ingredients together.

For a more cheffy take; Pour the bloody Mary into a pan and gently sprinkle over the powders, whisking all the time and bring the mix to the boil.

Prepare a tray lined with cling film then pour the boiling mix onto the tray so it is about 2mm thick, put in the fridge, it will set very quickly.

For the crab ice cream; Warm the milk then add all the other ingredients.

Put in the food processor and blend until smooth.

Pour the mix into a canister and freeze.

For the Henderson's Relish purée; Empty the Henderson's Relish in to a bowl sprinkle in one tablespoon of ultratex and gently mix with a whisk.

Ultratex will thicken without heat and will not lose its shine.

For the pickled cucumber; Warm the vinegar.

Add all the other ingredients and leave for 1 hour to infuse.

Peel and slice the cucumber into 1cm slices.

Cover with the liquor and leave to rest for 1 day.

For the crab; Mix the crabmeat, creme fraiche and coriander together.

Season with salt and lemon juice.

To assemble; Cut the jelly into sheets 15cm x 20cm.

Place on to cling film, put 100g of the crab along the long length.

Mould into a sausage shape.

Pick up the cling film, roll into a sausage so the two edges of the jelly meet.

Tie each end then leave in the fridge to firm up.

To Serve; Use four lightly chilled plates.

Place four smears of the hendos purée on the plate.

Cut each end from the crab cannelloni with the cling film on.

Remove from the cling film and put the cannelloni on the plate.

Place on two pieces of the cucumber.

Put the crab ice cream through your ice cream maker for one final churn or whisk from frozen out of the freezer.

Put a quenelle of the ice cream next to the crab.

Finish with some salad leaves.

RUPERT ROWLEY - FISCHER'S OF BASLOW

Fischer's restaurant has become the pièce de résistance of Baslow Hall, Derbyshire, thanks to foundations built by owners Max and Susan Fischer and the subsequent work of current head chef Rupert Rowley, who joined them 12 years ago.

The restaurant was awarded a Michelin star under Max Fischer in 1994 and has retained the honour ever since.

SMOKED BACON HASHCAKE
WITH FRIED DUCK EGG

THIS DISH CAN BE ENJOYED SEVERAL DIFFERENT WAYS, AS A BRUNCH DISH,
SUPPER DISH, OR IF YOU HAVE A HEALTHY APPETITE THEN AS A STARTER. YOU CAN SWAP
THE INGREDIENTS AROUND AS IT'S A BIT LIKE BUBBLE AND SQUEAK.
YOU COULD ALSO USE THESE CAKES AS A GARNISH FOR ROAST GAME. SERVES 4

INGREDIENTS

400g mashed potato

12 rashers smoked streaky bacon

1 large white onion

4 large red spring onions

Fresh thyme

Bunch of fresh chives

Flat leaf parsley

Bunch of lovage, optional

½ tsp ground cumin

Plain flour

Rapeseed oil

Salt & pepper

100g butter

4 duck eggs

For the ketchup

250g fresh gooseberries

1 tsp Henderson's relish

1 large white onion

150g caster sugar

100g dark brown sugar

150ml red wine vinegar

½ tsp ground mixed spice

1 clove garlic

Spring onion, for garnish

METHOD

To make the cakes, lay the bacon out onto a greased flat baking sheet and bake in the oven at 180°C for about 15 minutes until crispy. Remove and leave on the baking sheet to cool. Peel and cut the onion in half and slice thinly, place in a saucepan with a drop of oil, a few leaves of picked thyme leaves and a touch of salt and pepper, sweat the onion with a lid on for about 30 minutes until they are soft and translucent, remove from the heat and cool. Thinly slice the spring onions. Chop the chives, parsley and lovage if using. Place the mash in a mixing bowl, drain any liquid off the sweated onion and add to the mash with the herbs, spring onion and cumin. Take 8 rashers of the cooked bacon, chop into lardons and add to the mash. Mix it all together and season with some black pepper and a little salt if needed. Divide the mix into 4 and make them into cakes using a dusting of flour. They should be big enough to sit the fried duck egg on. Place them on a tray and put in the fridge until required, they can be made well in advance.

To make the gooseberry ketchup, peel and chop the onion, pick the stalks off the gooseberries and place all the ingredients in a large saucepan, bring to the boil and then simmer for about 1 to 2 hours or until the gooseberries become a shiny chutney consistency. Blitz the cooked gooseberries in a food processor and pass through a sieve. Pour the ketchup into a squeezy bottle.

To present the dish, shallow fry the hash cakes in some rapeseed oil and a good knob of butter, cook for about 4 minutes on each side until they are golden brown. Fry the duck eggs in a little oil and a knob of butter, place the egg on top of the cake in the centre of a plate, warm the remaining 4 crispy smoked bacon rashers. Garnish with the ketchup and some sliced spring onion.

JAMES MACKENZIE - PIPE & GLASS, EAST YORKS

With a history dating back to the 15th century, the Pipe and Glass Inn stands at the entrance to Dalton Park in Beverley, East Yorkshire.

Since 2006, the restaurant has been owned by James and Kate Mackenzie – who have lovingly overseen the restaurant's transformation into a Michelin-starred venue, adored by critics and customers alike.

CHERRIES FOUR-WAYS WITH HENDERSON'S ICE CREAM

THIS HIGHLY-SKILLED BEAUTIFUL DESSERT REALLY SHOWS THE CREATIVITY
OF THE CHEFS USING HENDERSON'S RELISH

INGREDIENTS

For the Henderson's Relish syrup

250ml Henderson's Relish

50g sugar

For the cherry purée

³/₄kg cherries

50g sugar

For the salted caramel cherries

¼kg cherries

50ml cream

50g butter

50g sugar

Sea salt

For the Ovaltine ice cream

250ml cream

250ml milk

12 egg yolks

180g sugar

2 tbsp Ovaltine

For the shortbread

175g self-raising flour

50g rice flour

1 tsp baking powder

100g sugar

100g butter

METHOD

To make the puréed, leathered and for the poached cherries; place cherries in a pan with the sugar

Once the cherries have softened remove around a quarter of them and set aside.

Blend the remaining in a food processor until smooth, then take half of the purée and spread on a greaseproof mat and cook for a few hours in a low oven until dried out.

For the Ovaltine ice cream

Slowly heat the milk and cream in heavy-bottomed saucepan.

Meanwhile whisk the egg yolks and sugar until light and fluffly.

Combine with the milk/cream, whisking continuously and to cook until the egg taste has gone then whisk in the Ovaltine.

Chill in the freezer, then churn in an ice cream machine, or in a freezer whisking every hour or so until frozen.

For the shortbread

Mix all the ingredients together until it resembles bread crumbs.

Place in a lined tray and bake on 200°C for 15-20 minutes or until golden.

For the salted caramel cherries

Place the sugar in a saucepan and heat to make a caramel, then add the butter and cream, whisking continuously.

Carefully, place the cherries in the hot caramel and coat, add a pinch of sea salt to each cherry.

For a Henderson's Relish syrup put the relish in a saucepan with sugar and boil to make a thick syrup.

LEE MANGLES - SILVERSMITH'S RESTAURANT

Self-proclaimed 'selectors of fine Yorkshire ingredients', provenance is Silversmith's raison d'être.

For owner Justin Rowntree and head chef Lee Mangles there's nothing more important than sourcing locally – a blueprint given to them by mentor Gordon Ramsay following their participation in his Kitchen Nightmares series.

And, of course, hand-in-hand with local comes seasonal. The cyclic nature of Silversmith's menus showcase the best of the best of local produce, from hearty beef pies to sumptuous rhubarb desserts, rich local cheeseboards and everything in between.

Mark MUSGRAVE

CLOTHING INSPIRED BY A CONDIMENT IS NOT SOMETHING YOU SEE EVERY DAY.

Mark studied Graphic Design & Photography in his hometown of Scunthorpe, later moving to Sheffield in 2008 where he started his business degree at The University of Sheffield. Through living in the city, he quickly developed an appreciation for the many local independent businesses and talented artists. As you can imagine, it was only a matter of months before he was introduced to delights of Henderson's Relish. Mark currently works part-time for The Level Collective – a Sheffield based clothing company who pride themselves on creating unique, ethically made products with assistance from some of the finest emerging illustrators, graphic designers and typographers.

The 'Strong and Northern' t-shirt design came from Rich Wells – one of the company's talented designers. It encapsulates two passions shared by many Sheffielders: Henderson's Relish and cycling. In keeping with the local emphasis, the original design was hand screen printed in Sheffield before being placed onto one of their ethically made organic cotton t-shirts.

www.thelevelcollective.com

STRONG
AND
NORTHERN

JON MCCLURE'S
CHILLI CON CARNE

IN THE WORDS OF THE REVEREND "EASY AND REIGHT NICE".
SERVES 4

INGREDIENTS

500g extra lean minced beef

1 Spanish onion, diced

1 tbsp vegetable oil

300g chopped tomatoes

400g passata

2 tsp cumin

1 tsp cinnamon

1 tsp chilli powder

2 fresh chillies, de-seeded and sliced

1 beef oxo cube

1 pinch celery salt

1 pinch ground black pepper

Glug Henderson's Relish

METHOD

Heat the oil in a large saucepan.

Add the minced beef and diced onion to the pan fry until golden brown.

Once the meat is fully browned, add the rest of the ingredients and stir well.

Turn the heat down and simmer for at least an hour.

Keep simmering until you are ready to serve.

If you like it spicy, do not remove the seeds in the chillies and it'll give it a good kick!

Serve with fluffy white rice, chips, or both!

Photo: Timm Cleasby | www.thepicturefoundry.com

JON MCCLURE - REVEREND & THE MAKERS

Jon McClure grew up in the northern suburb of Grenoside. After attending Notre Dame High School, he graduated from the University of Sheffield with a degree in history. Early in his music career he fronted local bands Judan Suki and 1984, later going on to form Reverend and The Makers in 2005, with the band's debut album 'The State of Things' reaching number five in the UK Albums Chart. Jon, or "The Rev" as he is affectionately known, has always been considerably vocal about his passion for Sheffield Wednesday FC and, of course, Henderson's Relish!

Yorkshire Brisket with HENDERSON'S GRAVY

Ingredients

500g brisket
6g star anise, blitzed
5g cumin seeds, roasted and blitzed
Sea salt, pinch
25g beef dripping
400g mirepoix (carrots, onion, leek, celery and garlic)
1 tsp tomato purée
125ml red wine
50ml Henderson's Relish
1 litre beef stock
1 bouquet garni
For the flat iron steak
400g flat iron steak
Olive oil, drizzle
Sea salt, pinch
10g butter
Freshly ground pepper
For the carrot purée
300g orange carrots
25g butter
200ml carrot juice
Sea salt, pinch
For the crispy fried onions
150g banana shallots
100ml milk
100g self-raising flour
For the pickled onions
200g sugar
25g salt
250ml white wine vinegar
250ml water
250ml beetroot juice
3 shallots, peeled and sliced
½ tsp peppercorns
2 star anise
Parsley and dill, stalks only
Sprig thyme
Olive oil
For the horseradish potato
250g Maris Piper potatoes
25g butter
50ml cream
1 stick horseradish

Method

Season the brisket on all sides with the star anise, cumin and salt.

Heat the dripping in a hot pan; add the brisket carefully to the dripping and fry until golden brown all over.

Remove from the pan and set aside. In the same pan add the mirepoix and slightly brown then add the tomato purée and cook out for 2 minutes.

Add the red wine and reduce by half.

Add the beef stock and Henderson's Relish, bring to the boil and pour over the brisket, then add the bouquet garni.

Cover with greaseproof paper and then a double thickness of foil.

Place into a hot oven at 180°C and cook until tender, approximately 1½ hours.

When cooked, remove carefully from the braising liquid and keep warm.

For the Henderson's gravy

Pour the braising liquid into a pan and reduce.

Check the seasoning and pass through a fine sieve and keep warm.

For the flat iron steak

Season the flat iron steaks with salt and freshly ground pepper and olive oil.

Place the steaks into a hot pan and leave to cook for 2 minutes on each side.

Add the butter at this stage and cook for a further 2 minutes.

When cooked, remove from the pan and allow to rest, then thinly slice.

For the carrot purée

Peel and slice the carrots and place in a pan with the rest of the ingredients. Bring to a boil, then reduce to a simmer and cook until tender, drain off the liquid and place the carrots into a food processor and blend until smooth.

For the crispy fried onions

Peel and cut into rings approximately 2mm thick, separate the rings and remove the centre ones.

Dip the rings in the milk and then the flour to coat. Place into the frying basket and shake off any excess flour.

Plunge into hot oil at 180°C and fry until golden brown then drain and lightly season with sea salt.

For the pickled onions

In a pan lightly sweat the shallots in a little olive oil.

Add the rest of the pickling juice ingredients and bring to a gentle simmer.

Pour over the baby onions, the acidity of the juice along with the heat will gently cook the baby onions, cover the tray and allow to cool.

For the horseradish potato

Bring the peeled potatoes to the boil and cook until tender, then drain and mash with the butter and cream. Grate the fresh horseradish into the potatoes, but don't add too much as a little goes a long way.

TIM BILTON - THE SPICED PEAR

Born and bred Yorkshireman, Tim Bilton, first made his name at The Butchers Arms in Hepworth – turning the venue into an award winning restaurant in just five years. Motivated by the challenge of running an independent, family owned restaurant, he opened the Spiced Pear Hepworth on Sheffield Road in May 2013. The venue houses a stylish restaurant, vintage tearooms and cocktail bar, and has already established itself as a firm favourite on the Yorkshire food scene.

MUSHROOM MERINGUE WITH
SUMMER FRUITS

TALENTED IRISH PASTRY CHEF, STEPHEN MCFARLAND, HAS CREATED
A WONDERFUL DISH USING HENDERSON'S RELISH.

INGREDIENTS

For the meringue

3 egg whites

170g caster sugar

4 tsp cocoa powder

For the glaze

150g caster sugar

50ml water

50ml balsamic vinegar

2 tbsp Henderson's Relish

For the garnish

18 raspberries, halved

18 blackberries, halved

9 strawberries, quartered

100ml fresh cream, whipped

Micro basil, for garnish

METHOD

Preheat the oven to fan 110°C.

Line two baking sheets with non-stick liner or parchment paper.

Place the egg whites into a large clean mixing bowl. Beat them on medium speed with an electric hand whisk until the mixture resembles a fluffy cloud and stands up in stiff peaks.

Now turn the speed up and start to add a tablespoon of sugar one at a time. Continue beating for 3-4 seconds between each spoon of sugar. It's important to add the sugar slowly at this stage as it helps prevent the meringue from weeping later but don't over-beat. When ready, the mixture should be thick and glossy.

Next spoon the meringue into a piping bag fitted with a plain medium nozzle. On one tray pipe 12 mushroom stems and on the other tray pipe 12 discs about 5cm wide.

Dust the discs with cocoa powder and place both trays into the oven for 1 hour until baked crisp. Remove from the oven and leave to cool.

For the glaze, place the sugar, water, balsamic vinegar and Henderson's Relish in a small saucepan and bring to a boil. Cook until reduced by half and a syrupy consistency. Transfer to a small bowl and set aside to cool to room temperature.

To assemble, place the mushroom stem in the middle of the plate, next place the round disc on top. Arrange the summer berries around the plate and pipe the dots of cream, top with the micro basil. To finish, drizzle the Henderson's glaze over the berries.

STEPHEN McFARLAND

Stephen started cooking at just 9 years old when he went to his Grandfather's every Saturday morning to make bread and pancakes.

In 2010 he went to work for Neven Maguire in Mac Nean Bistro, in Blacklion, Co. Cavan, Ireland. An Award winning, fine dining restaurant, with Neven being a renowned chef all over Ireland, working alongside him as Head Pastry Chef.

Stephen has had the pleasure of working in LA at Gordon Ramsay's restaurant, as well as New York, Dubai, London, and Abu Dhabi; being granted the opportunity to also work with Jamie Oliver.

CHOCOLATE COURGETTE CAKE

A DELICIOUSLY MOIST AND DARK CAKE - PERFECT WITH COFFEE.

INGREDIENTS

For the cake

Knob of butter

300g self-raising flour

3 medium eggs

100g golden caster sugar

200g light brown sugar

1½ medium courgettes, finely grated

2 tbsp Henderson's Relish

110ml vegetable oil

100g dark chocolate

40g cocoa powder

For the ganache

175g dark chocolate

1 tbsp golden syrup

100ml double cream

METHOD

Preheat the oven to 150°C. Grease a 20cm circular baking tin with butter. Roll out a length of absorbent kitchen towel and place the grated courgette onto the roll to absorb some of the water content.

Combine the Henderson's, vegetable oil and golden caster sugar with the courgette in a bowl, leave for 20 minutes to allow the courgette to soak.

Add the brown sugar, melted dark chocolate and eggs to the courgette mixture. Once fully combined, sift and fold in the self-raising flour and cocoa powder.

Pour into the tin and bake for 40 minutes – or until the point when a skewer just comes out clean when inserted into the cake.

Transfer cake to a cooling rack.

In a bowl, over a pan of boiling water, gently melt the dark chocolate for the icing. Once all of the chocolate is melted, stir in the golden syrup and gently beat in the double cream. If you're feeling adventurous use a splash of Henderson's! Using a spatula or palette knife distribute the ganache over the top of the cake and allow to cool.

TOM DRAKE

Tom is currently a medical student and researcher studying at the University of Sheffield. Due to the proximity of the old Henderson's factory to the University, there's never a lack of relish in the kitchens, naturally leading to attempts to put it into everything he creates – including desserts!

HENDERSON RELISH
The Spicy Yorkshire Sauce

Warp Films
10th Anniversary Special Edition

For That Extra Flavour With Film
MADE IN SHEFFIELD FOR 18 YEARS

Water, Spirit Vinegar, Sugar, Colour-Caramel,
Cornstarch, Acetic Acid, Cayenne Pepper, Cloves,
Tamarinds, Garlic Oil, Emulsifier-Tragacanth and
Alcohol, Containing sugar and artificial sweetener

...7384 (Sheffield) Ltd, Leavygreave Road, Sheffield

Luke
PREST

HENDO'S MAN IS OUT-THERE PROTECTING THE INNOCENT
AND SPICING UP THE BLAND!

After studying art at A-Level, Luke Prest originally intended to continue his education at university but instead accepted a job in an architectural practice. For the next ten years he didn't pick up a brush, until encouragement from family and friends motivated him to give it a good go. Since then, Luke has picked up a strong reputation as a local artist. He's been commissioned by the likes of Sheffield United FC, The Leadmill, The Sheffield Cook Book and he's even sold works to the Duke of Devonshire!

Luke's affection for Henderson's deepened with age as he grew to realise the uniqueness of the brand. His youthful fascination with superheroes caused him to create 'Hendo's Man', who is part of a larger superhuman allegiance sworn to protect the values of Yorkshire life. His job is simple but noble: help those in need of Henderson's. When Hendo's man nips around with a few bottles for Luke, he uses it to spice up a stew or splash all over his chips.

www.lukeprest.com

Adventures Of HENDO'S MAN

Only one man can help him.

Crisis! I'm out of Hendo's!

After a days graft, all Steve wanted was a splash of Hendo's on his Steak and Kidney

From his not very secret HQ - Hendo's Man swoops into action.

is it a bird?

is it a plane?

No! Its Hendo's Man!

Cheers Hendo's Man!

He delivers a bottle of Sheffield's finest and leaves Steve to tuck into his pie!

Sausage
CASSEROLE

A GOOD SAUSAGE CASSEROLE IS ONE OF THE MUST-HAVE DISHES WITH HENDO'S!

INGREDIENTS

4 sausages

3 large carrots

2 sticks celery

1 small onion

1 tin chopped tomatoes

4 medium potatoes

½ beef stock cube

1 tsp Italian herbs, heaped

½ pint water

Henderson's Relish to suit

Salt and pepper

METHOD

Preheat the oven to 220°C.

Peel the carrots, cut lengthwise and cut into chunks.

Cut celery into large pieces and chop the onion.

Cut each sausage into 3 pieces.

Add the sausages, carrots, celery, onion and tomatoes to a large casserole dish and stir.

Add the stock cube, herbs and water and stir until all has combined.

Add 3-4 shakes of Henderson's Relish and stir.

Add salt and pepper.

Place in the oven on the middle shelf for 2 hours.

Peel and halve the potatoes and add to the casserole then cook for a further 30 minutes.

To serve sprinkle with chopped parsley and eat with crusty bread.

BREFNI & JOHN SZLAUER – ST ALBANS.

John is a verger at St Albans Abbey and Brefni is retired from working in Social Services in Hertfordshire. Brefni's brother introduced them to Henderson's when he escaped north and since then they have been converting new recruits to the Henderson's cause through presents of Henderson's and their cooking.

Brefni's sausage and Henderson's casserole is featured here as their favourite and they hope will soon be yours.

STEAK
BURGER

A JUICY STEAK BURGER IS MORE THAN A MATCH FOR ANYONE.

INGREDIENTS

1kg mince beef (good quality 85-95% meat)

200g white onion, finely diced

25g beef stock cube

50ml Henderson's Relish

15g fresh parsley, chopped

5g fresh thyme, chopped

5g fresh rosemary, chopped

150g tomato paste

1 egg

Black pepper to taste

METHOD

Gently warm the Henderson's Relish, add the stock cube and stir until dissolved.

Add the rest of the ingredients apart from the mince and combine.

Add the mince and mix until it all looks the same colour and is fully combined.

Divide into 8 and shape into burgers, ideally press into a pastry cutter or ring.

Cover and allow to chill for 2-3 hours.

Either grill or pan-fry for approximately 4 minutes on either side.

Place a slice of cheese on top and allow to sit in the pan for a further 2-3 minute to rest.

To serve, place in a bun with and garnish with cheese, tomato ketchup, tomato slices, lettuce, bacon and a couple of large onion rings.

DANIEL NUTT - THE SITWELL ARMS HOTEL

Originally dating back to the 18th century, The Sitwell Arms Hotel in Renishaw has gained an excellent reputation for its high standards of service, accommodation and, of course, food. The chef team at the hotel's Wild Boar Restaurant are passionate about using fresh, local ingredients to create innovative and tasty dishes.

Richard HAWLEY

THE SHEFFIELD LEGEND HAS LOVE FOR A BOTTLE OF THE BROWN STUFF.

"There are things that define a city; there are also things that can unite or seriously divide a city. You also get things such as rubbish architecture which can try to hide what a city is really about. Sadly, Sheffield has the latter in great abundance, although I'm told there have been steps taken of late to correct this. Either way, good or bad buildings can't hide what is really ace about Sheffield: its people and its parks, the Peak District and the odd pub, too! On the whole, we are friendly folk – unless we're talking about football, of course. There's always division (and literally, a whole division this season) between Wednesday and United supporters. Speaking of seasons (or should that be seasoning?) there's one thing that defines and I daresay unites us all; that's Henderson's Relish."

Richard Hawley speaks fondly of his affection for Henderson's brand. He was of course the first real 'name' to go public with his love for the sauce. Hawley found fame as a member of 90s Britpop band Longpigs, before later going on to join fellow Sheffielder Jarvis Cocker in Pulp for a short period. Those early days of relentless touring with Longpigs during the height of their fame took their toll on Richard, and he recalls how the taste of Henderson's Relish helped him to settle in upon returning home.

"I spent most of the 90s on tour somewhere in the world and got to the point where I couldn't even remember my name at times. I'm not knocking it – it beats working for a living, you know what I mean? Anyway, I got back from being in the States with the Longpigs for nine months and was in a mess. When I finally got home, I just walked into the house and sat down. My wife had cooked tea for when I got in and I sat there, and didn't speak or anything. She put the plate in front of me – sausage and mash and gravy, with Hendo's on. I took one mouthful and burst into tears – the taste of Henderson's was the one thing that proved to me I was home at last."

Richard would later go on to demonstrate his talents as a solo artist: releasing seven studio albums, and embarking on a number of successful tours. Famously, his self-titled first album had its launch party in the yard of the old Henderson's factory, although details have always been scarce – due to the lack of photo evidence from the evening in question. A photo booth was set up to take a picture of each guest with a bottle of Henderson's, but camera film issues meant that only half of the pictures ever materialised.

Other than photograph issues, the rest of the event went without a hitch. As the guests mingled in the yard, Jarvis Cocker – who had offered to DJ so he could see the inside of the factory – provided the entertainment by spinning a few tracks from the decks.

However, Richard's working relationship with the brand didn't end there. In 2005, Richard commissioned his own specially labelled bottle to promote the release of his Mercury Prize nominated album, 'Coles Corner'. Fans were able to purchase the limited edition bottles after live shows, and the move proved so popular that Hawley released another commissioned label upon the release of his following album, 'Lady's Bridge'.

The Sheffield crooner has always remained loyal to his roots, and can often be seen around the city centre – sometimes nipping for a pint in Fagan's pub or heading to the shops to stock up on his favourite spicy condiment. Richard, like many others in the city, accepts Henderson's Relish as a part of daily life for Sheffielders – a constant feature of the family life which has been passed down through generations.

"There are not many Sheffield households I've been to which don't have at least one bottle in the cupboard. All of my family love it. I tell my sons, 'That'll put hairs on thi chest that will, kid.' Funnily enough, I've never said that to me daughter! I hope people enjoy this cook book as much as our city has enjoyed Henderson's Relish for well over a century."

SHEFFIELD SECRET
MIXED GRILL

THE SECRET? WELL THE KEY INGREDIENT HAS BEEN MADE IN SHEFFIELD FOR OVER 100 YEARS. SOME SECRET EH!

INGREDIENTS

4 Sheffield Secret Bacon Chops

4 Sheffield Secret Beef Burgers

4 Sheffield Secret Sausages

400g potatoes, skin on

2 tomatoes

2 large field mushrooms

Oil spray

4 eggs

Henderson's Relish

Salt

Vinegar

BEECHES OF WALKLEY

Chris and his wife and business partner, Donna, have worked hard over the last few years to develop their inner city farm shop 'Beeches of Walkley', supporting many local independent businesses from breweries and farms to condiments and honey makers and also many of the farmers market stall holders.

METHOD

Preheat the oven to 220°C.

Remove any blemishes or 'eyes' from the potatoes then slice lengthwise into thick rectangular chips, leaving the skin on.

Bring a large saucepan of salted water to the boil. Add the chips and blanch for 10 minutes. Drain then leave aside for 10 minutes to dry.

Meanwhile, cut the tomatoes in half and remove the stalks from the field mushrooms.

Place all the meat under a moderate grill and cook to your liking.

Return the chips to the dry saucepan, cover with a lid and shake to 'rough up' the edges of the chips – this roughness is important to the texture of the chips.

Spray a metal baking tray with oil spray. Transfer the chips to the tray, spray lightly with cooking spray and bake in the oven for 20-25 minutes, turning occasionally, until golden brown on all sides.

Place the mushrooms and tomatoes alongside your meat under the grill, then cook until the tomatoes are softened and the mushrooms are lightly browned.

Make your poached eggs by whisking a saucepan of lightly simmering water into a whirlpool. Drop the eggs, one at a time, into the centre and add a few drops of vinegar to the water to stop the white breaking up.

Arrange all the meat on a platter, with the chips, and then place the tomatoes, mushrooms and eggs on top.

Alternative to including chips, why not garnish with fresh watercress or other leafy green salad to provide a contrast of colour. Boiled new potatoes and peas are good accompaniments to this dinner

Lastly if you think there may not be enough Henderson's in the meat ingredients, then feel free to add lashings of the relish for flavour.

SLOW-COOKED OX CHEEK

RICH AND DELICIOUS - A REAL WINTER WARMER.

INGREDIENTS

2 ox cheeks, sinew and excess fat removed

½ white onion, peeled and sliced

1 carrot, peeled and sliced

1 celery stick, sliced

2 sprigs fresh thyme

2 plum tomatoes, halved

1 large glass red wine, merlot is good for this recipe

1 small glass Madeira

400ml beef stock, enough to cover the cheeks

Salt & pepper to season

Lots of Henderson's Relish

Olive oil

METHOD

Pre-heat the oven to 180°C.

Season the cheeks generously with salt and pepper, then heavily brown them in a hot casserole pan with some good quality olive oil.

Remove them from the pan and set aside.

Now brown all of the vegetables in the casserole pan, then set aside.

Pour in the red wine, Madeira and thyme, reduce the liquid by two thirds and then immediately remove from the heat.

Now add the vegetables back to the pan and then the ox cheeks and cover with the rich beef stock. Put a lid on the pan then place in the pre-heated oven for around 3 hours, making sure you turn the ox cheeks half way through cooking.

Remove from the oven, let it cool slightly and then remove the ox cheeks from the pan and set aside. Pass the remaining liquid through a fine mesh sieve in to a clean heavy based pan and rapidly reduce the liquid to a nice thick glaze-like viscosity, remove from the heat and add a good few glugs of Henderson's Relish and stir it in.

Whilst the cheeks are still hot brush the glaze all over them generously and serve with, mash and cauliflower cheese plus more Henderson's Relish!

FANCIE

First opened in 2007, Fancie grew to become a household name in Sheffield with their ethos of "great food, great cakes and great people" resonating strongly with local food lovers.

The popular Ecclesall Road store recently came under the ownership of Matt Bigland – who also own the successful Milestone and Wig and Pen gastropubs in the city.

James COATES

THIS STILL LIFE REALLY BRINGS OUT THE HENDO'S.

"If you cut a man from Sheffield, he will probably bleed Henderson's," claims James Coates. After leaving school, James broadened his horizons by travelling extensively for a number of years. Upon his return to the UK, he came to visit friends living in Sheffield. Like many before him, James fell for the City's charm and stayed put. He spent a few more years studying law at Sheffield Hallam University and The University of Sheffield, eventually becoming a solicitor. After realising the job didn't suit him, he returned to his lifelong passion for art and began painting again.

James likes to paint objects found around the house and, naturally, a bottle of Henderson's is never far away! The use of a linen canvas provides a smooth surface, which helps to add an edge of photorealism to the painting. Oil paints were preferred as they allowed the artist time to hone the detail of the piece whilst the oils took time to dry.

CLIFF HOUSE
MUSHROOM STACK

EVEN IN WALES, THESE EXILED SHEFFIELDERS STILL KEEP A GOOD STOCK OF
HENDERSON'S RELISH IN THEIR CUPBOARD.

INGREDIENTS

1 slice good granary bread

Mushrooms, thinly sliced

1 tomato, baked

Handful Cheddar cheese, grated

Henderson's Relish

Sprig of parsley

Tomatoes, to garnish

METHOD

Cut the tomato into half and bake in the oven for 8-10 minutes.

Thinly slice the mushrooms then gently fry until golden.

Toast the granary bread. When in Wales we prefer to use Laugharne granary, but in Sheffield Roses wheaten bread would be ideal.

Cut the toast into a ring using a non-stick poaching ring.

Place the baked tomato on top of the toast, press down and then sprinkle with Henderson's Relish.

Spoon on the cooked mushrooms to fill the ring. Sprinkle with a little more Henderson's Relish.

Cover with grated cheese then place under a hot grill until the cheese is bubbling.

Using a spatula transfer the stack to a plate, remove the ring and garnish with tomatoes and a sprig of parsley.

CLIFF HOUSE GUEST HOUSE, PEMBROKESHIRE

After many happy years of living in Sheffield, Anne and Michael Slade moved to their B&B, Cliff House Guest House on the Welsh coastline in February 2010.

They were keen to serve breakfasts that use local produce as well as reflect their heritage and love of Sheffield.

Henderson's Relish was the perfect ingredient to combine with good Welsh produce and from this they invented 'The Cliff House Mushroom Stack'.

Visiting Sheffield friends keep them supplied with relish and many of their guests from all over the world are now converts to Henderson's Relish.

MARINATED STRAWBERRIES
WITH PISTACHIO CAKE

A GREAT TWIST - SERVING HENDO'S WITH CAKE!

INGREDIENTS

For the strawberries

200g strawberries

100ml water

130g sugar

2 tsp Henderson's Relish

For the pistachio cake

250g butter, room temperature

250g sugar

250g pistachios, ground

50g flour

25ml rum

5 eggs

Small handful pistachios, to decorate

METHOD

Wash and hull the strawberries (by removing the green stem).

Quarter the strawberries and place in a bowl.

Place the water and sugar in a saucepan and bring to the boil. Once boiling, lower the temperature and cook for a minute or so until the mix has thickened slightly.

Pour the Henderson's Relish onto the strawberries.

Cover the bowl with cling film and allow the strawberries to steep in the cooling syrup.

Preheat the oven to 170°C.

Place the butter and sugar in a bowl and whip until light and fluffy.

Then 250g pistachios in a food processor and blend until you are left with a light powder, put this to one side.

Add the flour to the cream and butter mix, and fold in.

Beat the eggs and then add a little at a time and fold into the mixture.

Add the ground pistachio nuts and rum, and fold through into the mixture.

Grease and line an 8" round cake tin with baking paper.

Place the mixture into the cake tin and bake at 170°C for 40 minutes. To test place a skewer into the centre of the cake and ensure the skewer comes out clean. If there is residue on the skewer, cook for a little longer.

Allow to cool on a wire cooling rack.

To serve, slice the cake and place onto a plate. Spoon over a few of the strawberries and then drizzle with the Henderson's Relish syrup. Sprinkle with a few chopped pistachio nuts and serve with cream or ice cream.

JAMES WALLIS - ROOM RESTAURANT, MANCHESTER

James grew up in Sheffield and learned his craft with Henderson's Relish always as a staple household ingredient.

In this unusual twist Henderson's is paired with strawberries as a dessert. Think strawberries with balsamic and black pepper and it's not too far a jump to use the spicy relish in this delicious dessert.

He currently heads up Room restaurant in Manchester.

HENDERSON

RELISH

The Spicy Yorkshire Sauce

Made in Sheffield for over 100 years

For that extra flavour with
meat, fish, soups, pies, casseroles
and vegetables